Empower your kids!

A coaching guide for parents

The ultimate guide for coaching them to overcome low self-esteem, anxiety, anger, fear of failure and much more with NLP, EFT and 25 years experience!

BY JUDY BARTKOWIAK

First published by Free Association Books.

A CIP Catalogue of this book is available from
the British Library

ISBN: 978-1-911-38356-7

Typeset by
Typo•glyphix
www.typoglyphix.co.uk

Cover and illustrations by Jane Kelly

Printed and bound in England

For parents everywhere, you are amazing.

These extra coaching skills will enhance what you already do, give you new ideas and ways to guide your child to where they need to be, emotionally and mentally.

Contents

PART 2

Introduction

In 2010 I wrote my first book '*Be a happier parent with NLP*' which was based on everything I had learnt about applying Neuro Linguistic Programming to parenting my own four children and working with children and teens in my coaching practice 'NLP Kids'. I followed this book with a series of workbooks called '*Engaging NLP*' which were written for children, tweens, teens and parents, to learn about and to apply these NLP techniques and ways of thinking for themselves. I then went on to train others in NLP and then, in 2018, I trained in the Emotional Freedom Technique and Matrix Reimprinting. So this book '*Empower your kids! A coaching guide for parents*' is an update, which includes everything I have learnt in the last 10 years as well as the experience I have gained through training and coaching.

Much has changed in our reading habits and the way we access parenting information, so I have deliberately tried to make this book a blend of theory and practice with plenty of practical activities you can do with your children, together with a few examples that I hope will illustrate the idea.

In Part 1 you will discover how NLP and EFT can add to your existing parenting skills. It is a general section that is relevant to whatever your child or teen may need right now. It is a good starting point for understanding how we process what we experience, from our initial response, what we make something mean based on our unique mind and then what we do with this in terms of behaviour. Here you will also find the 'how to' for EFT tapping although I will include a short reminder in chapters where I've suggested tapping so you don't have to keep turning back to Part 1 every time. It is more of a reference section which you may want to refer to if you find something you'd like to know more about as well.

In Part 2 you'll find the topic chapters. I've tried to think about all the different situations or issues you might encounter, but please be aware that I am not a doctor so I'm purely giving you some ideas based on NLP and EFT of things you can try yourself. If I've missed out something you want to know more about, in the first instance find something similar and use that chapter, but you could also contact me for further help. I would say that in any situation, tapping will relieve any negative emotions and is uniquely versatile - your child simply says what they feel and you can help them tap through the points and clear it.

One of the core premises of NLP is that you already have all the resources you need, and I fervently believe this. One of the resources you quite definitely have, and may not fully appreciate, is your intuition.

My intention with this book is to give you a 'go to' for whatever you feel is troubling your child. If you're not sure, a good question to ask yourself is, "if I was behaving in this way, what would I be feeling?" This child is your child, they are 'of you', they have learnt from you so use your instincts and your understanding of yourself to understand them. It's a good starting point. This will lead you to the chapter in this book that you need to use with them.

I have four grown up children now but they weren't always grown up. NLP and then EFT gave me tools and techniques to use to understand them and to calm myself so that I could more clearly make decisions, communicate them and hold fast. Needless to say, it is much easier, as any coach or counsellor will tell you, to help other people's children than your own. Many times they would say, "Mum, don't NLP me!". But they've all grown up to be wonderfully wise and kind so I'm going to guess that NLP certainly played a part in that.

A bit about me: I am a prolific writer and loved writing even as a very small child, writing squiggles on paper made into tiny books for my dolls and reading them the 'stories' I'd written. I also love teaching, too. I love to share what I know about working with children and teens which is something I've been doing since I left University, first as a Children's Qualitative Market Researcher and then as an NLP Kids'

Coach, more recently adding other modalities such as Art Therapy, Mindfulness, EFT, PTT and Walking Therapy into the mix. In this spirit of sharing, I ask you to share these tools and techniques with your children and your families.

The principle behind this book of coaching skills is that as parents we want to step in and help our children but sometimes this verges on rescuing when we take over and do things for them that they could do themselves. When they work out a solution for themselves this builds confidence and resilience, and it teaches them that confidence comes through learning from mistakes and making different choices, seeing new possibilities. By rescuing we deny them this learning experience. Coaching puts the onus back on them to take responsibility and when you learn these coaching skills you'll know just what to do and say to encourage them.

PART 1

NLP

Basic Principles

'Neuro Linguistic Programming' doesn't exactly trip off the tongue, does it? Luckily, it's a lot easier to explain than it is to say.

'Neuro' is everything in our mind: our thoughts, beliefs about the world we live in and beliefs about ourselves, those we love and who matter to us, and others with whom we interact. It is our experiences and memories. In fact, there are so many million pieces of information in our heads that we have to apply some filters to reduce those thoughts to a manageable amount that we can cope with! It refers to the way each of us processes what we see, hear, feel, taste and smell. We experience something through our senses and we filter it through our life experiences, memories, beliefs and values such that every one of us creates, from that same experience, something unique which we call our internal representation.

The 'Linguistic' part is how we express that through our body language and the words we use, our tone and everything about the delivery of our language. Each of us has a style or preference (visual, auditory and kinaesthetic and within that a preference in terms of our metaprogrammes (choices/process, detail/concept, towards/away from, match/mismatch) so we each convey what we are thinking in a different way. When we want to be heard and understood by our children, it helps if we have some awareness of our child's language patterns so we can match them for rapport. I'll explain all of these so you can work out your own language pattern and that of each of your children.

'Programming' is the result and the patterns we run. By noticing the structure of each interaction, we can make better choices so that we can improve the communication next time. We can fall into patterns of behaviour which do not give us satisfaction, yet we often find ourselves repeating them just because they are familiar. It is our challenge to question and change these patterns so we can get the results we want and be happier as a parent.

I explain this sequence to children when I first meet them and they find it interesting to think about some of the things that happen to them on a regular basis, break it down and work out what they need to do differently to get a different result. I only wish it was as easy as this; it does take a few sessions!

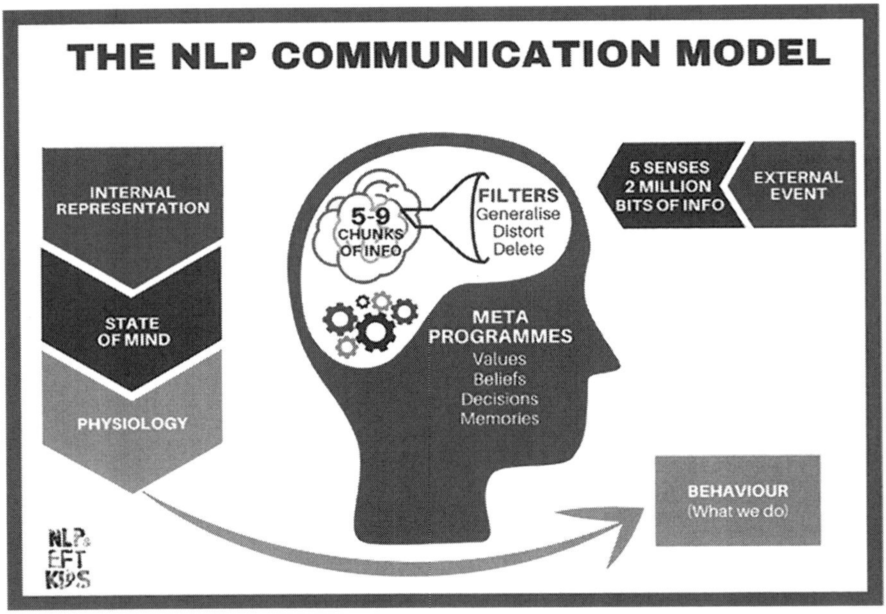

The emphasis of NLP is on what happens *before* the behaviour. As parents we often find ourselves focusing on the behaviour. That's what we notice first. But what about the things that went on in your child's head to produce that behaviour? What about those thoughts, feelings, memories and experiences that created beliefs about themselves, some positive and others less so, that made them respond with that particular behaviour? When we only focus on the behaviour, especially the behaviour we don't want, we miss the opportunity to help them change it by understanding the process for themselves and choosing different options.

The Emotional Freedom Technique or EFT is an energy healing technique based on rebalancing the energy flow in the body through tapping on meridian points. This is expressed really well in this diagram.

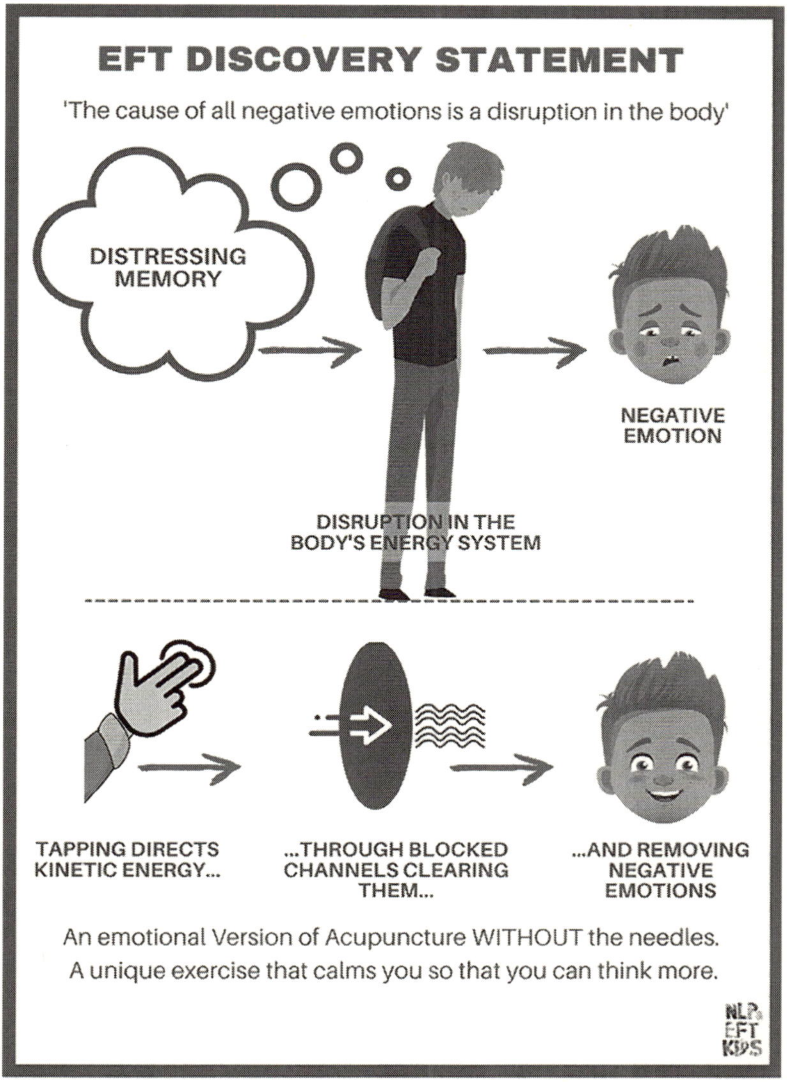

We are their 'people of influence', they love us, watch us and learn from us, so I want to share with you how YOU can influence the changes that you want to see in your children simply by learning about how we all process our world.

In Part 1 I'm going to explain how NLP and EFT applies to parenting and give you the opportunity to try the techniques for yourselves first. Maybe practise them on your partner. Become familiar with the thinking behind the techniques so you feel comfortable with them and you'll soon get the hang of how to use them so fluently that you can just introduce them to your child or teen as they need help, in the moment.

How to improve connection and understanding with your children

If you've heard of NLP before it may have been through work. A lot of companies use elements of NLP in their training programmes to enhance management and leadership skills. Of course, as parents this is what we are doing with our children. I well remember listening to Sue Knight talking about how NLP can be used to motivate employees and my immediate thought was "I wonder if this would work to get my kids doing their homework without moaning?" It did!

We need to be amazing managers, leaders, motivators, counsellors, first aiders, teachers, chefs, party planners... and whereas the needs of employees may change year on year perhaps, the needs of our children can change weekly. So, we need to be creative, versatile and able to give and receive feedback constantly so that we can better adapt to a changing environment.

What I used to find so hard, though, was the emotional involvement. We love our children and are acutely aware of our responsibility to raise them in the best way possible. This isn't like the work environment at all, is it? Every failure, every success is personal. It can't *not* be. Yet, sometimes, it is the fact that we take everything personally that can get in the way of making the best decisions and responding in the most 'adult' way. We can let our emotions get the better of us and end up sounding more like a child than the child themself.

One of the most useful NLP techniques I applied successfully was **disassociating**. Imagine when you are right in the middle of it, feeling their pain, feeling your own pain, and unable to think clearly. Now take an emotional step away for a moment and imagine the scene as if from an impartial bystander or even a CCTV camera. What do you see now, what do you hear? When we do that, we focus on what we observe rather than our interpretation of the situation which has become clouded by our emotion as a parent.

I will take a brief dive into Transactional Analysis here to explain. We have access to three modes of being:

Parent – all the 'should's, 'must's and 'ought to's

Adult – the computer mind, slightly detached, observes and reports

Child – the emotions: love/hate, passions, joy/sadness, overt expressions of emotion

At any time we can be in one of these modes, as can your child. I'm sure we've all heard a child tell another child what they 'shouldn't' do. When we get into a shouting match with our child, we are both in 'child' mode. At some point, we may move into 'parent' mode and tell them what they 'must do' but disassociating is to step into 'adult' and to observe what's happening, what's being said, what is needed, and to calmly ask questions to seek resolution.

This section here is about 'skilling you up' so you have more choices of how to respond to your child. My belief is that the more choices you have, the more chance there is of one of the choices being effective.

Let's start with understanding ourselves. When we know ourselves better, we have the tools and vocabulary to understand our children.

Thinking back to how much we experience every moment, imagine if we had to process each of the many millions of bits of information individually each time we saw, heard or felt anything? In order to reduce the amount we have to process we focus more on the senses we prefer.

These senses are **visual (see), auditory (hear), kinaesthetic (feel)** (known as VAK), olfactory (smell) and gustatory (taste). Most of us can access them all quite easily but at different times we will focus more on one than another.

We do tend to have a preference, though, so if you usually notice what you see, care about how you look, the colours you wear and the visual aspects of your surroundings then you may well be visual. You will notice messy bedrooms, things not being in the right place and probably have a creative flair.

Is this you?

If your child tends to be more visual, they will notice your facial expressions, how you look, how their food looks and in a general way, colour, form and the way things appear to them. They will want their writing to be neat and not want to cross things out and they will learn best from what they see, so diagrams, pictures and the written word will be good learning tools for them. Their voice tends to be higher and they speak fast, looking up as they access images in their mind. They tend to be very imaginative so dreams can be vivid and sometimes frighteningly real and for that reason too, they can often imagine the worst-case scenarios.

Maybe you are auditory, you love to chat, take a call rather than text, love music, notice sounds?

Is this you?

An auditory child will focus much more on what is said, what they hear and how you speak to them, picking up on tone of voice and volume, pitch and pace. They will tend to process a bit slower than a visual child, listening much more carefully to the words and thinking about what words they want to use themselves. They often have a lower pitch than a visual child. Auditory children notice noise and sounds, so creaky floorboards, the TV on nearby, raised voices and extraneous noises near them in the classroom will be distracting. They need to control the noise around them. They will want to talk things through and have things explained slowly and they tend to remember what you say.

Or, do you tend to be a bit fidgety, find excuses to get up and move around? You may notice being too hot or too cold, certain fabrics irritate your skin and you love to be active. You may want to be physical, touching someone's arm when you're talking to them, hugging them and wanting to sit close to someone. You notice the atmosphere in a gathering and are sensitive to how people feel around you.

Is this you?

A kinaesthetic child is all about the body, movement, touch, temperature and feeling the atmosphere. They find it difficult to be still and enjoy being active. The feel of clothes and other textures may irritate them as will being overly hot or cold. They will want to feel comfortable rather than look good. Kinaesthetic children learn through doing, through working it out for themselves. They want to do, rather than see or hear so school can be a challenge if they have to sit still for a long time. For obvious reasons, they tend to be the most sporty children. They also find sitting in the classroom quite difficult because they want to be moving.

It's a good idea to know your own child's preference so you know what they will be most likely to notice and focus on in any given situation. It will help you to match your language pattern to theirs. It will help them to engage with what you are saying if they can immediately connect with the pattern.

Visual connecting words are: look, see, watch, notice, imagine, picture

Auditory connecting words are: sound, hear, listen, noise, speak, chat, say, tell

Kinaesthetic words are: touch, feel, go, get, find, do, make and any action words

By using their language, you make it easier for them to know what you're asking. Be curious, what words are you hearing from them? Yes, each child may well have a preferred pattern and yes, you can combine all three VAK into one sentence. For example, "Did you hear me (auditory), just look at the time (visual) you need to get into bed, and fast(kinaesthetic)!"

Use this opportunity to note what pattern each of your family use:

....

Just when you think you have this, I want to add in another element of language pattern, and that is the **metaprogrammes**. These are different ways of processing our world. Imagine each one as a continuum. We ideally need some flexibility to be anywhere along the continuum depending what we need to do, but, in reality, most of us have a preference, rather like with VAK and tend to favour one end or the other. Knowing which your child favours will indeed help you decide how to communicate with them. Regardless of which of the specific chapters you want to turn to first, you will need to communicate with your child, so, understanding which metaprogrammes they are running will help enormously. It will also help to know which ones you are running because as with VAK, when we find ourselves operating a different pattern of communication to our child, it will be like speaking another language and your child will need to translate what you say into their pattern in order to understand what you want. Easier, surely, to simply use their pattern and minimise potential for miscommunication.

Choices/process

It is a mistake to think that <u>all</u> children want choice. We read that we should give them choice in everything but that isn't always what they want.

Some children want 'process'. This is like a tick list; do homework, eat, play games with friends on my phone, shower, bed. They work through a list and having a choice or options simply gets in the way and can even confuse them. I've actually had parents ask me if there's something wrong with their child because they get confused when asked to choose between different things.

Children who like 'choices' get lots of enjoyment deliberating on which of the options they will take. The longer they can draw this out, the better. They like to choose clothes, menu options, films and so on. Removing choice from them will annoy them, even cause them to be angry. So if your child likes choice, but they can't have a choice, then you need to create a choice within the process. So for example, they want a choice about whether or not they have to do their homework, you can instead offer them a choice of where to do it, when to do it, which subject first, which snack to eat while doing it.

Be aware of your own position on this. You will tend to offer choices if that's important to you but, if you are more inclined to the 'process' way of thinking, maybe you won't even think about there being a choice at all. Now of course if your partner is one and you are the other you will probably be very aware of the difference. I'm speaking from personal experience here!

Who is 'choices' and who is 'process' in your family?

....

Match/mismatch

Does your child look for what's similar, what's familiar, what's the same? Do they find change and new experiences difficult? Do they respond badly to surprises? Do they want to know what to expect ahead of any activity? This is a 'match' child. They tend to connect easily with other children, eager to find things they have in common. They like to agree and they will avoid conflict, even agreeing to things they don't really want to do rather than experience difference or discord.

A 'mismatch' child however will thrive on disagreement and look for what's wrong in what you say. It's easy to take such a child as being argumentative, difficult or deliberately trying to annoy, but this isn't the case. They thrive on difference and constantly seek clarity and want things to be 'just right'. Such children tend to have a scientific brain and, as you might imagine, fit well into careers where knowing what's wrong is important such as doctors, lawyers, engineers, scientists. This is called 'a yes but' pattern for reasons that will be immediately obvious to you if you have a 'mismatch' child. If your child often responds with a 'but' they are mismatching.

You may notice this if you have one sibling wanting to 'match' and another wanting to 'mismatch'. The 'matching' sibling can feel hurt and take it personally that their sibling keeps suggesting different games, wants to watch different videos and doesn't agree with them. Help them to understand that it isn't personal; it's just the way their sibling's mind works and they aren't deliberately being difficult or critical.

You can help your 'mismatch' child by encouraging them to think about how people are similar or how your idea is similar to theirs, and you can help your 'matching' child by encouraging them to notice difference so they know it is fine to disagree sometimes and to follow their own path when someone suggests something they don't agree with.

Who is 'match' and who is 'mismatch' in your family?

....

Towards/Away from

A 'towards' child will be focusing on what they want and this certainly makes it easier for the brain to process their instructions. They are naturally positive and looking to what they want to achieve, how they want to be and what they want to have; be it friends, more pocket money, more screen time and so on. The opposite of this is 'away from', which means that they tend to focus on what they don't want. Imagine the confusion for your 'towards' child if you were to suggest they should do their homework to 'avoid getting into trouble' when they hadn't even considered this.

What an 'away from' child wants is to avoid confrontation, being told off, getting into trouble, having no friends, missing a shot at goal and other undesirable things. In fact, they struggle to think about what they actually *do* want because their mind is so focused on what they don't want. This can result in them getting more of the things they don't want because they're so focused on those things that they are looking out for them all the time, to the extent that they miss what is right in front of them. They miss out on the things they actually do want, but they don't know what they are. You can help this 'away from' child by gently asking them, "What do you want?" You'll find it takes them a surprisingly long time to work it out. Don't prompt them, their neural pathways need to do a complete U-turn and this takes time. In doing the U turn, they are creating new possibilities and it's important they do this for themselves.

Who is 'towards' and who is 'away from' in your family?

....

Big chunk/small chunk

Some children like detail, they want to know all the facts, the plans, and what they need to do in the smallest detail. Other children just want the general idea and they can work it out and get it done. As I said, each of these ways of being is a continuum and 'chunk size' is a good example of this, in as much as children need access to both small chunk detail and big chunk concepts. So, even though they will have a preference, you can help them learn how to 'chunk up' and 'chunk down'.

When you deliver communication in the 'wrong' chunk size for your child they can easily find it overwhelming. A child preferring detail can be completely lost when given a 'big chunk' idea. So for example, "write about winter" as an essay title will be too vague and not mean anything to them. It offers too much ambiguity and they have no idea what to do. The 'big chunk' child however will be delighted at such an instruction and have lots of ideas. They might miss some of the detail though, such as grammar and spelling mistakes because that wasn't important to them.

To help your child 'chunk up' say, "Think about what this means," or "What's the end result?" "What's it all for?" "What's the point of the exercise"?

To help your child 'chunk down' say, "So what is the first step?" "What do you need to do?", "Write a list," "Make a plan"?

Who is 'big chunk' and who is 'small chunk' in your family?

....

Internal/external

In a nutshell, internal is 'I' and external is 'you'. 'Internally referenced children focus more on themselves, their own views and thoughts, with less awareness or interest in those of others. They tend to be single minded and uninterested in what others think of them. Externally referenced children do care, possibly too much, and are totally reliant on the views of others and unable to tune into what they themselves think. They are very co-dependent and likely to be easily hurt by unkind words in the playground.

How you can help here is to ask, "And what do YOU think?" to encourage the externally referenced child to check things out for themselves rather than take the word of others. To the internally referenced child you need to say, "And what did the others say?" to encourage them to be more aware of how their behaviour impacts others.

There are times of course when we need to be firmly focused on what *we* want as parents and then there are times we need to focus on what *they* want but it's good to check in with them and with yourself as well, because there's always another perspective. When we are open and can move up and down the continuum there is more chance of making a good connection with our children and them with their friends.

Who is internally referenced and who is externally referenced in your family?

....

Associated/Disassociated

I touched on this earlier, recommending that parents consider stepping away from a battleground and disassociate, and to see the situation without some of the drama and emotion, as an impartial observer. This gives us a calmer more authoritative stance, which will calm the situation and give us more chance of being heard. When both we and our children are in 'child mode' there is unlikely to be a good outcome. On the other hand, if we are too 'disassociated' we can seem like a computer, heartless and unfeeling.

Being 'associated' is therefore being totally <u>in</u> the drama and taking on the emotion of the other person. If instead it's done with a little detachment, it can be empathetic, rather than appearing to be more emotional than the other person who shared their story.

Who is associated and who is disassociated in your family?

....

Some metaprogrammes will be more pronounced in your children than others. There may be some that you don't even notice because they move fluidly along the continuum. This is the ideal situation where they have that flexibility. The metaprogrammes you notice most are likely then to be where there is less flexibility.

Note these here for each child.

....

....

....

As you think about the chapter you want to turn to, and about the issue that is at the forefront of your mind, ask yourself: how could this issue be being affected by my child's metaprogrammes?

....

....

So now let's break it down so we can understand what goes on in our child's mind when we say or do something.

I'm going to take an example of you saying "It's time to go to bed now."

1. They **generalise**

This is when we make the one example true in every case for example when we use words like 'everything', 'everyone', 'no one', 'always', 'never'.

Imagine if we had to process each of the many millions of bits of information individually each time we saw, heard or felt something? This would be too difficult and time-consuming, and so we generalise, we put the thought into a category with other similar experiences or events. We make assumptions that this is similar, so we don't have to treat everything as if it's the first such situation. For instance, we see a queue and we know that when we see a line of people, we fall in behind because that's what we do. We don't have to wonder what to do each time, because otherwise everything would take a very long time for us to process.

However, when we group experiences in this way, we treat it as a fact. In fact, how many of us, seeing a queue, think we should join it? When children present generalisations to us, they do sound like facts, don't they?

A type of generalisation we often encounter with children is

And one we use ourselves perhaps?

Stop yourself when you use such generalisations because, just as you know your child's generalisations to be untrue, they know yours are too so they ignore it.

2. They **delete**

This is when we make a statement that, like the generalisation, lacks evidence or context.

Here's an example where there is no context.

Better than when? Better than whom? In what way better?

We can only learn from feedback that has the specifics, so we know how to process it, how to do better next time.

3. Then they **distort**

This is when we mindread or predict the future. I remember doing this on many occasions!

Your children do it too, of course.

I expect many of you recognise some of these phrases.

What are the things you say? Can you think of any generalisations, deletions or distortions that come to mind as you've just read this section?

Write them here

....

....

Now re-write them without generalisation, deletion or distortion.

....

What about the children. What do they say that are examples of generalisations?

....

Your response to a generalisation could be

- Really?
- Everyone?
- Always?

The response to the 'I can't...' is

- What's stopping you?
- Who's stopping you?
- What will happen when you do it?
- How will you feel when you've done it?

The replacement for should/must/ought to is

- I/we want you to...........

Own it.

Generalisations are rarely true. Do it with a smile and you stay in rapport yet still make your point.

How do they delete the context?

....

When children express opinions as facts or make meaningless comparisons such as later, earlier, better and so on, you can gently ask them for evidence as to how they know this to be true.

- In what way better/fairer/easier, etc?
- According to whom?
- Who says this?
- How do you know this is true?
- Interesting, tell me more?

What will they have predicted or how might they have thought they could read your mind?

....

Children may think they can read your mind or that they know what will happen but they can't and they don't. You don't set out deliberately to annoy or upset your child. We have a choice as to what we take their behaviour to mean as they do ours. Rather than argue or repeat ourselves, it works better to simply ask the question,

- How do you know this?
- How did I/she /he do that?
- How do you know this will happen?

So, after generalising, deleting and distorting what happens next?

We run through our beliefs, values and historic experiences of similar situations and from this we create our own internal representation of the event, the thing we have experienced through our senses – seen, heard, done, smelt or tasted.

I'm going to start with **beliefs** because they are so important and frequently misunderstood. In normal parlance we use the word 'belief' when we talk about religious belief and these tend to be rather fixed. They are also very general and universally understood. In NLP when we talk about 'belief' we mean 'what I hold to be true for me right now about a certain specific situation or thing'. The difference here is that NLP beliefs refer to beliefs that are very personal to us and based on our own map of the world, no one else's. Also, they change with time, with new information and with intervention, such as coaching.

What are your beliefs about parenting?

What is a 'good parent'?

....

....

What would you like to do more of as a parent?

....

....

What would you like to do less of as a parent?

....

....

Who is your model of a 'good parent'?

....

One of the things I say to children is:

"Control your controllables"

You cannot control what your children do or don't do. The one thing you can control is your own thoughts, beliefs, expectations – what you say and do and how you respond to them.

What could you do differently as a parent that might help your child with whatever they are struggling with right now?

....

....

How we respond to our children is based to a large extent on our values, the moral code we live by and what steers our life path. Our values will be more global than our beliefs and will be shared by our friends and family in most cases. We pick up our values from our parents and we seldom change them. Sometimes we are only aware of our values when something happens to shock and upset us because it goes against those values. We might get annoyed by people with different beliefs about the world we live in, but when values are different this is more of a problem because it touches us at our core.

Think about your family values. What are they?

....

....

Experiences, memories and decisions will alter our beliefs but not our values. In the case of your children, the sort of experiences and memories that will affect them will be the birth of subsequent children and the impact on their position as centre of your universe, death of grandparents, significant changes such as separation and divorce, major operations involving a hospital stay and starting school.

Have a think about the key events of your child's birth to the age of 6yrs and the belief or decision they may have made at that time. Is there any way there is a connection between that belief and the belief that may be behind the behaviour or issue you are currently thinking about?

What have been the key events for your children? They will be different for each child, remember.

....

....

All of these filters in our 'neuro' combine to create our internal representation of what we experienced as the external event. Others experiencing the same external event may well have different internal representations.

This results in a state or mood – it could be surprised, annoyed, happy, etc. and often children can't name what they feel. For this reason, it might be called 'anxiety' but each child experiencing what they call 'anxiety' will be referring to their own specific, personal, internal representation, based on their own unique experiences in life and memories.

Our state is represented in our physiology (body posture, expression on our face) and if it is not clear, try and match the body language and expression and ask yourself, what would I be feeling if this was my physiology?

Next is the behaviour. We say or do something as a result of the internal representation, the state and the physiology.

This then becomes the next 'event' and so the process continues.

Remember that you are an external event. What you say and do is your child's external event so you have a measure of control in this area. How you express what you want to happen will have a major impact on your child's behaviour. I hope in this last section you have gained a better understanding of how you currently communicate, how your child communicates and how you can make some adjustments to create a better connection and understanding.

How to have a positive mindset in parenting

It would be useful now to share with you the NLP Beliefs of excellence. These are the beliefs that John Grinder and Richard Bandler created as a code for excellence. They researched the 'difference that makes the difference', in other words, what beliefs, when held, make the difference between achieving one's outcome or not achieving it. That outcome could be anything. It could be something simple that you want to do, like getting your child to bed with ease, getting them to school on time or their homework being done. It's tempting to add 'without a drama' but what we do there is create an 'away from' outcome where we focus on what we don't want – drama. What you focus on is what you get more of. It's sometimes called the Law of Attraction. It's about what we put out there in our 'energy field'. Children understand this idea. They know very well that what they expect to happen generally does happen, especially when it's something negative.

1. If you always do what you've always done, you will always get what you've always got

As parents we often find ourselves repeating the same words and actions hoping to get a different result. Maybe occasionally we do actually get the result we want, but mostly we don't, and yet we continue in that hope that the success will be repeated. We get in a rut because what we are doing is something we did with the last child, or something a friend recommended or something we read in a book (like this one) or this was the way we were brought up ourselves. There's almost certainly a good reason behind it, it isn't just random.

Yet, despite the fact that it isn't working, we continue. Maybe we blame ourselves, maybe we blame them or we blame 'the situation', whatever that might be at the time. But there's no need to find someone or something to blame. Just do something different.

Do it in the spirit of experimentation, of curiosity, with a positive intention to create the best possible communication with your child.

Remember to focus on the outcome you want, think about 'towards' and what you DO want to happen.

2. There's no failure, only feedback

As a parent, I remember feeling like I was a failure plenty of times. I didn't tend to feel it about my work, but the relationship with your children is so much more intense. We are more 'associated' with them and there almost isn't a boundary between us, emotionally. Work is transient and we move from job to job in a much less intense fashion. We are more disassociated and this makes the difference. When our child feels something, we feel it too, so we can feel responsible when they struggle in life, and we want to fix whatever is wrong for them. It's easy, then, to feel a failure.

But what if you could reframe this and see it simply as feedback that you can do something about. When your child needs help, this isn't a reflection of your skills as a parent, just an opportunity to be curious about how to help them.

It's the same for children who fear failure, encourage them to see it as an opportunity to think differently, to do something different. If we didn't fail and make mistakes, how would we learn and develop?

We may feel foolish or disappointed in that moment of 'failure' but when we look back on it, we realise that it needed to happen for us to move on and make changes.

I find the word 'just' helps here. When something goes wrong, reframe it as 'just a mistake', 'just a wrong turn', 'just a bad grade'. We can always do better next time.

3. There's a positive intention behind every behaviour

This belief is also about being curious and having a positive attitude. When something happens that you find annoying or upsetting, be curious and wonder what your child's positive intention might be.

Start perhaps by thinking about when you yourself did or said something similar. What was behind that? We all have a deep need to be seen, heard and understood, and when we feel we are not, there is hurt, anger, frustration and pain. How we express these emotions may not make sense to others but it is done with the positive intention of communicating a need that feels unmet in that moment. Your challenge as a parent is to discover what that need might be and how to meet it.

4. If you spot it, you've got it

Think about those you admire. What it is about them you admire?

Who is it?

....

What is it about them that you admire, find inspiring?

....

And in what way are you also like that?

....

Yes, you'll find that because you've noticed a quality or gift in someone else, you have it too in some area of your life. Be curious and find it. This is a super question to ask children as well. There's an exercise in my book *Understanding children and teens: a practical guide for parents, teachers and coaches,* called the Superhero exercise. It asks children to draw themselves as a superhero and there's a list of great questions to ask them, all designed to elicit, in an indirect way, the skills and gifts they themselves have.

But it works both ways. Those things you don't like in others might be your own 'shadow'. How do you have those traits?

Think about something one of your children did recently that annoyed you.

Who was it and what did they do?

....

In what way did it annoy you?

....

And in what way do you do something similar?

....

And when you do that, what is your positive intention?

....

Could this also be theirs?

5. The map is not the territory

This is so important when we think of communication between parents and children.

Let's face it, it was a while ago when we were children and a lot has changed, their world is quite different from ours and as you've just been learning, each of us processes our world completely differently.

For a start, their world is a whole lot smaller. For them, family and close friends, their teacher and carers are their world. Home and school are the only places that are important. So any changes within this territory of theirs will have a huge impact, especially if they are children who 'match' and look for things to stay the same and seek familiarity.

When we judge their responses from our map of the world, we will not understand them. We need to step with curiosity into their world and ask them how it is for them rather than guess.

Questions like, "What's it like when...?" or "What do you think when...?" or "What would you like to have happen?" are all what we call 'clean questions' which come with no assumptions or judgements. Even cleaner questions would be "Tell me more" or "Can you explain?"

This is about perceptions and it will help children become more emotionally intelligent when you encourage them to also see things from your point of view. When you do this, remember to avoid mindreading, telling them what you think they meant. Use a cleaner version instead, such as, "It sounds to me as if..." or "I'm feeling a bit... Is that what you intended?" Or I sometimes use this one, "Do you want to have another go at saying that as it sounded a bit... to me". Children don't have our verbal skills and sometimes come out with things they don't mean to, or use words thoughtlessly or incorrectly, so give them a chance to repeat what they said in a way that you understand.

You cannot *not* communicate. Sometimes we feel hurt by what our children seem to be saying without checking out whether that was what they meant.

We communicate with our face, our body, our eyes, everything. Our voice, tone, pitch, volume, even our silences, all communicate. I sometimes think less is more with children. When we are talking, we aren't listening.

6. We already have all the resources we need

Amazingly, I've found this to be true! We already know how to copy others. We've learnt this from birth. We used to watch our mother and father around the house, listen to how they talk to each other, watch their facial expressions, how they did things like eat, and this is how we learnt to walk to talk and to understand what was going on, how to behave and how to respond.

Later, at nursery school and at primary school we learnt how to learn, we learnt how to communicate using words and actions, and we learnt how actions had consequences.

Through copying, through learning, reading, listening to those around us and those we see on television, in YouTube videos, podcasts we listen to, books we read, we gain resources that we can use in our world.

I find parents often forget that the skills they use at work, and the skills they use in their sports or fitness or hobbies are all skills and resources that they can use as a parent.

7. The person with the most flexibility controls the system

Imagine if you only had two piano keys or two keys on your computer keyboard, 'yes' and 'no', 'this' or 'that'. You'd have a very boring tune or email. The more options you have, the more opportunities there are to achieve what you want. There are so many different ways to communicate, and the best way is to match the pattern of the person you're speaking to so that they have the best chance to understand what you are saying.

Think about how you can say or do something differently, consider other options and invite your child to work out how they could do something differently or think about something differently. When we assume there is always a solution to every problem, we can then focus on finding that solution and take responsibility for it ourselves rather than expecting others to resolve it.

8. The mind and body are one

How we think and feel affects our body. If we feel sad or fed up, our body sags and almost folds in on itself. When we feel happy, our body opens up and we look up, we smile and face the world.

Did you know that we can also use our body to alter our state of mind?

Here are some fun exercises for you. Before you do each one, score your state of mind on a scale of 0-10 with 10 being really happy and zero being really sad. Then score yourself again afterwards. What was the difference?

- Run up and down the stairs a few times
- Run round the garden a few times
- Do a really huge belly laugh as you think of something funny you've seen
- Deep breathe in for 6 and out for 6 three times
- Do a super hero power pose

The fastest way to change your state is to change your breathing as the breath travels throughout the body, moving the energy around and creating 'flow'.

Now you know the key principles of NLP. You'll find NLP techniques in the chapters of Part 2.

EFT

Basic Principles

The Emotional Freedom Technique is usually referred to as EFT or more commonly 'Tapping' because that's what we do. You can do it alone or with a therapist like myself. You can also, importantly, do it with your children, which is why I have included it in this book. It is often referred to as 'acupuncture without the needles' in that it uses the body's energy pathways or meridians to rebalance the flow of energy that gets disrupted by negative emotions. This is the EFT Discovery statement showing you how it works.

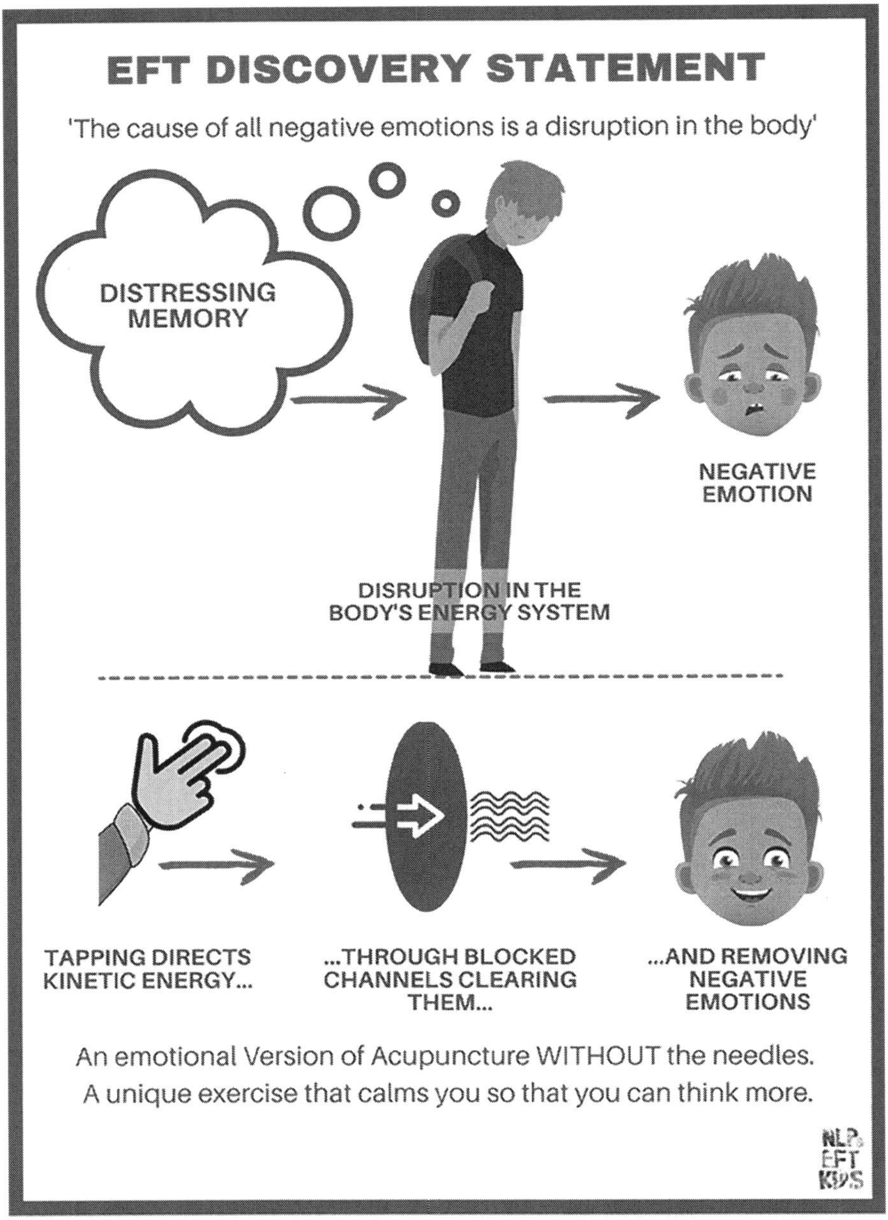
EFT DISCOVERY STATEMENT
'The cause of all negative emotions is a disruption in the body'
DISTRESSING MEMORY
NEGATIVE EMOTION
DISRUPTION IN THE BODY'S ENERGY SYSTEM
TAPPING DIRECTS KINETIC ENERGY...
...THROUGH BLOCKED CHANNELS CLEARING THEM...
...AND REMOVING NEGATIVE EMOTIONS
An emotional Version of Acupuncture WITHOUT the needles.
A unique exercise that calms you so that you can think more.
NLP EFT KIDS

I explain it to children like this:

> "You know how when things are going well, you sort of feel like you're 'in flow' then something happens, and you feel sad, or mad or bad and that flow sort of stops and you feel all sluggish and 'not in flow' anymore?
>
> Well we're going to tap on parts of the body and say the thing we were thinking about when that happened so we can clear that blockage and make it flow again.
>
> You might get an odd burp as that happens or you might find yourself yawning, that's all fine and it shows it's working."

Regular tapping keeps our energy flow moving and clears (this is the term we use) those negative emotions. Although tapping is considered by some as a bit 'out there' or 'woo woo' and mystical, its origins are extremely old, deriving from ancient Chinese medicine. It was discovered as an effective treatment for phobias by Dr Roger Callaghan in the 1980s. One of his students, Gary Craig, adapted it and simplified it for more mainstream therapeutic use in the 1990s and one of his students, Karl Dawson, trained me and thousands like me, all over the world.

Mindfulness was similarly viewed as being 'alternative' and is now part of most children's school curriculum, and so is EFT becoming more widespread as a tool for behavioural management and overall mental health in schools. There are many sound reasons for this which I'd like to share with you.

Remember in the NLP chapter I explained that we have to process millions of bits of information every day and have to filter it by generalising, deleting and distorting. Many of these bits of information have memories attached to them from experiences we have had in the past.

Test this for yourself. When you think back to your childhood, was there anything that you might describe as a 'bad memory'? Briefly write it down here.

....

When you think of that memory, what emotion comes up?

....

If there was a belief or decision your younger self made, in that moment, what was it?

....

Do you find that this is an issue you see in your life today?

....

How could this be affecting your parenting?

....

What happens is that our subconscious created a belief about ourselves in the memory and also created an emotion. This happens, especially in the case of negative experiences, as a way to protect you. By allowing you to remember it, we can then hope to avoid repeating it. However, what often happens is because we are on the lookout for it, we inadvertently attract it. Something that would mean nothing to someone else will trigger us into a Fight/Flight/Freeze response. It's like re-experiencing that early years' memory every time. The emotion will seem quite child-like as a result. Whenever something happens that triggers that belief, or the memory, we also experience the emotion attached to it, such as fear, hurt or anger, and this sends a signal to our brain that causes an imbalance. We can release this with tapping. As we tap we say the words that relate to the negative emotion.

We can use tapping for any negative emotion and it is very fast and effective for calming children from babies to teenagers. It is also extremely beneficial when we, as parents, tap on ourselves so we can stay calm, resourced and be the best version of ourselves. So, start by having a go yourself. Practise on yourself. Practise on your partner and your friends. One of the best things about this technique is that when you're helping someone else you don't even have to know the situation that has triggered them. You can clear the negative emotions without them having to share the back story.

How to support your own wellbeing with tapping

Let's start with you.

As parents we need to feel confident that we know what we're doing, rather than following our notes (although of course you can do that as well) and we want to assure ourselves that it works. Please be open to this because I promise you that it works and it works fast. Also, the person tapping does not even have to believe it will work.

The magic of EFT is that we can deliberately focus on the feeling and then tap on the meridian points to help rebalance the body's energy system. Maybe you have found that parenting can bring to the surface old hurts from your own childhood: things you'd wished your parents had done or said, things you wish they hadn't done or said. We can find ourselves being judgemental, rigid about rules, being fearful and over protective, or overly confrontational when we don't mean to be.

Was your childhood a happy one?

....

Think about what you liked about the way you were parented.

....

....

What would you like to change about how you parent your own children?

....

....

What would you like your children to say about their childhood when they are grown up and look back on it?

....

....

There's no such thing as a perfect parent; we just all do the best we can given what we know and our own circumstances at the time. Your own parents did the best they could and you are doing the best you can. We make mistakes and we can learn from them and forgive ourselves, aiming to do better next time.

Use EFT yourself before trying it with your children because you'll find it will make a big difference. You will feel calmer and more in control of your emotions, start to recognise the triggers so you can tap and respond differently. Remember you can't change your children's behaviour, only your response to it. You can change how you communicate with them and I've talked a lot about that in the NLP chapter. The chances are that they will notice a difference in you. Many of my parent clients tell me that their children notice how much calmer they are after having been introduced to tapping.

You can introduce it to your child by telling them that you'd like to try a new relaxation technique with them that you've learnt. A good time to show them is at bedtime when they are able to focus completely on you and aren't trying to do something else. Maybe ask them if there's anything that happened at school that they feel sad or worried about and that you have a magic way to make it go away so they can get to sleep.

It's quick and simple so practise on yourself first so you can use it with them.

I want to introduce you to the tapping points first.

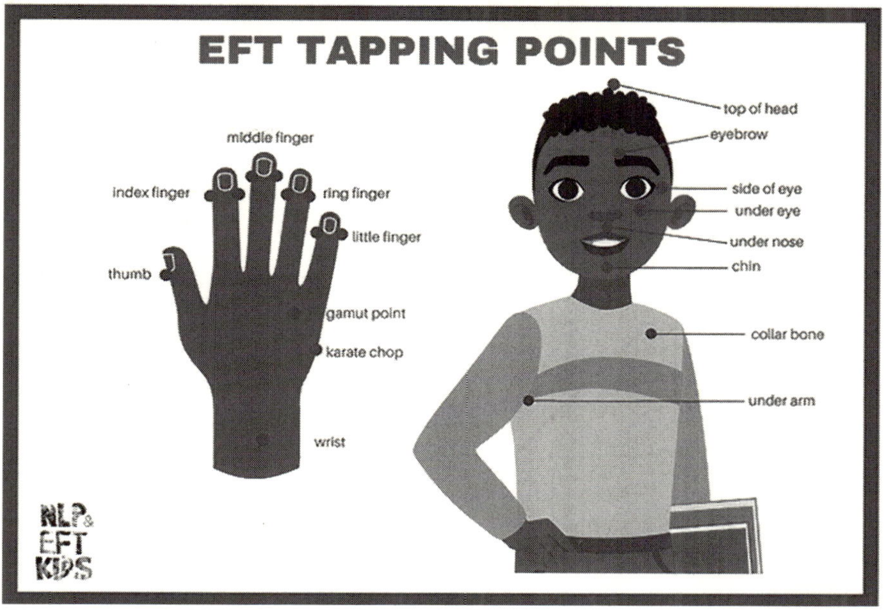

Let me take you through the process. I suggest you do it on yourself first time to familiarise yourself with the process.

Preparation

It's a good idea to have water to drink as any energy work we do tends to make us thirsty. You may also want tissues in case you get upset. Children tend not to get tearful because they find it easier, on the whole, to release emotions that build up, whereas we tend to squash them down. This means that when we do release, we may cry but these are healing tears and you'll feel much better after, I promise.

Now think of something you'd like to work on. It should be a specific event, occasion, situation, something said or done, ideally recently. Choose something that made you mad or sad. Start with something that is a SUDs level of around 4 or 5. The SUDs level is a scale of 0-10 where zero is 'no distress at all' and 10 is '100% distress', so less than half way. You can work on more distressing situations once you've practised on the smaller ones. When you ask a young child about their SUDs level you might find it easier for them to understand when you ask them to show you how big it is by comparing it to an animal. Is it as big as a mouse, a cat or dog, a horse, or a whale for example, or compare it to fruit; the size of a grape, an orange or a melon?

Step 1 – Tuning in

This is something you will need to do if you are not currently in the state you want to clear. Tuning in helps you re-create what you experienced earlier in the day perhaps. It's like telling our body, 'this is what we're going to work on today'. Aim to be as specific as possible so rather than say something like

> "I don't feel appreciated."

Think instead about a specific situation so

> "I didn't feel appreciated when I cooked a lovely dinner for the family this evening."

If you find it hard to be specific because it feels so overwhelming and it feels like it's everything and nothing in particular, you can simply tap on 'these feelings' or 'overwhelm' or even 'I have no idea'. The thing is that whilst your conscious mind may not have a clue, subconsciously there's a lot to process so we can leave our body's energy system to do the work for us and just use simple words like 'feeling rubbish' or 'can't cope' and let your body do the rest. This is called **global tapping** and it's how you tap in a classroom or in a group where people don't want to share their specific issues.

When you are currently in the state you want to clear then you can miss out the tuning in stage and go straight to the tapping. Similarly, with your child you can just tap on a general or global feeling.

Note down what you're working on ....

What is the SUDs level at the start ......?
SUD stands for 'subjective unit of distress'. We use this to calibrate how things are going and how much more work needs to be done.

a) We 'tune in' by
   - closing our eyes
   - putting our hands to our heart
   - breathing in, imagining you're breathing into your heart, for the count of four and out for four. Do this three times
   - thinking hard about the occasion, event, situation or whatever happened that triggered the negative feeling.

We want to bring it to our mind and body so we can clear it.

b) Now as you focus on the feeling, answer these questions. If you don't know, just guess because your subconscious mind will give you the answer. Note key words because you'll need them for the tapping. Our subconscious knows what our conscious mind cannot know because our feelings aren't always logical.
   - Where in your body do you feel it?
   - What colour is it?
   - What size – grape, orange, melon?
   - Hard or soft?
   - Is it moving or static?
   - What is the feeling?

Key words from tuning in

Where in the body? ....

Colour ....

Size ....

Anything else about it ....

Step 2 – Set-up

Tapping on the side of the hand which we call the 'karate chop' point, you say the following. When you do it with your child, they repeat after you, so you'll need to break it down into bite size chunks that are short enough for them to remember.

> "Even though I have this (colour) (feeling) feeling in my (part of the body), I love and accept myself anyway."

You say the set-up phrase three times, changing it each time to include all the information you have.

To give you an example, say if you have noted the following when you tuned into, for example, feeling sad about an argument with your son:

- In my tummy
- Green
- Orange
- Hard
- Static
- Sad

You would set-up by saying,

> "Even though I have this green sad feeling, the size of an orange in my tummy, I love and accept myself anyway."
>
> "Even though I have this hard, green, static, sad feeling in my tummy, I love and accept myself anyway."
>
> "Even though I have this green, sad feeling in my tummy I love and accept myself anyway."

Do you feel awkward saying "I love and accept myself anyway?" Some people do. If you do then change it to something similar that still conveys the feeling that you are OK despite feeling sad. I encourage children to say it because I think it's important that they do love and accept themselves unconditionally. Children so often focus on what they can't do and think others are smarter, more attractive, funnier and more popular than them so a little bit of self-love doesn't go amiss.

Options that you can use instead are:

"I am OK for now."

"I am a good boy/girl."

"I accept that's how I feel right now."

Step 3 – Tapping Rounds

We use reminder phrases here. The reminder phrases will just be words and phrases from the original set-up statement that you noted. If you're doing this as a practice for yourself you can obviously use whatever words come to you as you tap and your child can do the same.

Start with the top of the head and say one short phrase or word, then move to the next one as you go through the points. Tap about 6 or 7 times on each point gently. It doesn't matter which hand you use and you can change hands, or even use both hands if you wish.

We work our way down in this order

Top of head
Eyebrow point
Side of eye
Under eye
Under nose
Above chin
Collarbone
Under arm
Wrist

Go through the points, we call this *a tapping round*, twice.

Step 4 – Check back in

Go back to the side of the hand tapping on the karate chop point. This is an opportunity to check back on:

1. Has the feeling changed/ What is it now?
2. Colour, size, texture, moving, static, describe the new feeling
3. Where in the body is it now?
4. SUDs level

You may well find that the feeling has changed. As we tap around the body, we move the energy around and this clears one feeling but may replace it with another, different feeling. It is not unusual for anger to replace sadness or the other way around. What may have happened is that situations have 'aspects', different phases as the situation develops so just as this changes so too does the energy in your body so be prepared to tap on one feeling after another. Only repeat the set-up if the emotions take a significant change.

a) If the feeling has changed you should repeat the above process for another two tapping rounds using the new set-up phrase with the new information.

I sometimes move to tap through the fingers for the second set-up, partly to make a change and sometimes because changing the tapping points shifts more energy around. These are on the side of each finger, including the thumb, and the easiest way is to take the thumb and index finger of one hand (usually the dominant hand) and gently squeeze the nail point, either side of the nail, taking the nail and top of finger between the pincer movement of the thumb and index finger.

b) If the SUDs level has reduced and there's no change in the feeling other than it being less intense and probably a lighter colour, continue tapping maybe moving to tapping on the hand points.

Step 5 – Ending

Once the SUDs level is at zero, or 1 or even 2, and when you feel much calmer, happier, return your hands to your heart and breathe in for four and out for four.

Then think to yourself:

> "If there was a colour that reminds me of this nice feeling, what would it be?"

Then this is how we end the session, consolidating the work with a gentle breathing exercise.

> "Breathe in this colour into your heart and fill it completely with this colour. Take it through your body and into your (name the part of the body where the feeling was at the start) then back up to your heart filling it right up with this lovely colour."

You will find that even if you only got down to a 1 or 2, this last part of the exercise will take it to zero.

Make sure you drink plenty of water because any energy clearing work can be dehydrating and tiring. You might find that you yawn, or even burp, as the energy shifts.

How to tap with your children

You'll notice there are tapping points on the body and on the hands. The beauty of EFT, one of many in fact, is that it is really easy to teach children so they can use it themselves whenever they need to, even when we aren't around. They can therefore use it at school and instead of using the usual body tapping points they can use their hand points under the desk. Many schools have introduced tapping as a way to create a learning state for children at the beginning of a lesson and to ease anxiety and stress before exams or times of difficulty in class.

A lot of children struggle to get to sleep or they wake up at night and can't get back to sleep. This is an excellent technique to teach them because they can get themselves back to sleep.

The other aspect that makes EFT so great with kids is that we use very few words and those we do use come from them. It's useful to have a pen and paper to hand to jot their words down because it is important only to use the words they use. This is called 'Clean Language' and it means we use exactly what they say throughout the process. We don't correct or summarise or make any assumptions, the process is 'clean' in that we keep ourselves out of it and just follow the process.

I'm going to talk you through the basic process here so you have it to hand but having done it yourself already using my more thorough instructions you'll be able to make the minor variations needed for different issues mentioned in the chapters in Part 2.

If you have young children you can tap directly on them so they don't have to think about where to tap themselves. As they become familiar with the points, they can do it for themselves or they might like to tap on their bear or cuddly. This is what we call **surrogate tapping** because whilst you or your child is tapping on the bear, they're actually thinking of their own thoughts and projecting them onto their cuddly toy.

We can also do something similar when we tap for our loved ones. We can bring our loved one to mind and imagine we are tapping on them. If we get a really good connection, we can actually ease their stress even though they may not even know we are tapping for them.

Step 3 – Tapping Rounds

Now we start tapping through the points using some of the words they've used. Just check with them that the words are OK because as the energy shifts, so too do the emotions and they can change. I usually say:

> "If I say anything that isn't true for you any more or if the colour changes or where it is in the body, just let me know."

Tap 6 or 7 times on each point and say one of the words. You say it first and they repeat it. As they get the hang of it, they can say their own words. The idea is for them to be able to do this for themselves.

Start with the top of the head and say one short phrase or word, then move to the next one as you go through the points. Tap gently. It doesn't matter which hand you use and you can change hands, or even use both hands if you wish.

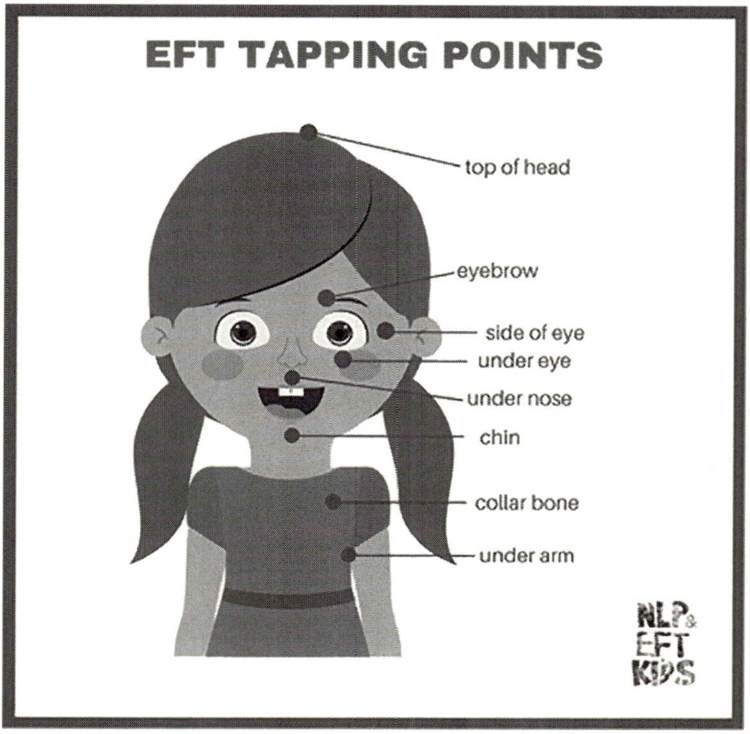

We work our way down in this order

Top of head
Eyebrow point
Side of eye
Under eye
Under nose
Above chin
Collarbone
Under arm
Wrist

Go through the points, we call this *a tapping round*, twice.

Step 4 – Check back in

Go back to the side of the hand tapping on the karate-chop point. This is an opportunity to check back on:

- What's the size of the feeling now?
- Has the feeling itself changed, if so what is it now?
- Where in the body is it now?
- Colour?

Remember that feelings change as different aspects of the situation or problem emerge. If the feeling has changed you should repeat the above process for another two tapping rounds using the new set-up phrase with the new information.

If the size has reduced and there's no change in the feeling other than it being less intense and probably a lighter colour, continue tapping maybe moving to tapping on the hand points.

Step 5 – Ending

Once the bad feelings have gone and when they feel much calmer, happier, return your hands to your heart and breathe in for four and out for four.

Then ask:

> "If there was a colour that reminds you of this nice feeling, what would it be?"

Then this is how we end the session, consolidating the work with a gentle breathing exercise.

> "Breathe in this colour into your heart and fill it completely with this colour. Take it through your body and into your (name the part of the body where the feeling was at the start) then back up to your heart filling it right up with this lovely colour."

Make sure they drink plenty of water because any energy clearing work can be dehydrating and tiring. Again, you might find that they yawn as the energy shifts.

While we're on the subject of tapping sequences and energy shifts, I'd like to share a little technique with you called **the 9 gamut procedure**. I'd say this is like pressing a reset button.

I teach this to children to use if they find themselves drifting off in a lesson or stuck on a question in an exam. It's like rebooting the mind, in a gentle but highly effective way.

Find the groove on the hand between the little finger and the ring finger of your non-dominant hand. Use the index and middle finger of your dominant hand to tap gently on that groove. As you do this you need to also:

- Open eyes
- Close eyes
- Drop eye gaze down to your left
- Drop eye gaze down to your right
- Circle eyes clockwise
- Circle eyes anticlockwise
- Hum a tune
- Count to 9
- Hum a tune

Now you should feel ready to help your children and introduce them to tapping.

One thing I'd like you to be aware of is that sometimes children resist clearing their worries and anxiety; this is called **Psychological Reversal**. What is blocking them from resolving their issue is what they will have to do as a result, or what they will *not* have to do.

For example, a child struggling with sleep issues who is getting a lot of attention (maybe negative attention) has got into the habit of getting the attention and isn't too keen to just go to bed and not see you until the morning. A child who gets help in new situations because of their anxiety, may not want to do new things alone. Here are the questions to ask:

- If there's an upside of having this problem what would it be?
- If there was a downside of not having this problem what would it be?
- Encourage them to think about this from another angle.
- What would the upside be if you didn't have the problem?
- What would you be able to do once this problem has gone?
- If there was another way of looking at this problem what would it be?
- What would a good outcome look, sound and feel like?

Here is a list of all the issues you can use tapping for with your child

- Fear of the dark, being alone at night, noises, burglars
- Back to school, changing schools, starting school, teacher problems
- Friendship issues, bullying, meanness
- Exams, performance anxiety
- Pain
- Eating problems
- Toilet training/ bed wetting
- Stuttering
- Fear of failure

How to tap with a baby

It's hard to know what's wrong with a baby so the best way of helping them is to tap on yourself because you'll be worried, frustrated, confused and in need of some tapping. Your baby will pick this up, so whatever you do for yourself, you do for them as well.

Here are some good set-up statements for this situation.

> "Even though my baby (say name) is crying/ not sleeping/ (name the situation) I'm a good mummy/daddy and I love her/him."

You say the set-up statements three times as usual. Then start tapping on your normal tapping points around the body. If you're in the same room as the baby you may not want to draw attention to yourself. Tapping on the finger points or the collarbone is a good one if you just want to tap gently and quietly. Ask your partner to tap as well, remember they don't have to be in the same room.

Now you can turn to the baby and tap for whatever may be troubling them. They may not want to be tapped on, especially if they're crying but if they're just restless or windy, you can just touch their hand points (but NOT the top of their head) gently and breathe quietly using a set-up statement such as:

> "Even though I'm restless/ tired/want attention/ have wind, I know my mummy and daddy love me."

Say this three times.

The stomach meridian point is just under the eye so if they're windy you could tap there using one hand very gently of course, two fingers (first and middle finger) so you do both eyes together.

If your baby is happy on their front, a good way to use tapping to calm them is to take two fingers, as I just described above, each side of their spine and tap gently from the base of the neck down to the coccyx.

If your baby had a difficult birth or if you didn't get the birth you wanted, you can specifically tap on this. Tap on yourself and say the set-up three times.

> "Even though we had a difficult birth/ didn't have the birth I wanted/ we are safe and well and I love you."

Many new parents feel overwhelmed by the responsibility of having a new baby and feel unsure what to do. It's not unusual to feel trapped and resentful. When we pretend we don't feel these things it's usually because we feel guilty or ashamed, and feel we should squash these feelings down. We don't get to release them. Tapping is one time when you can say how it feels to you. Find a quiet place away from the baby and your partner and tap on whatever negative feelings you have.

> "Even though I feel overwhelmed/depressed/angry/resentful/ trapped I know this is normal and it will pass."

You're going to do three set-ups so change the wording as you wish each time.

Be gentle and loving to yourself. Keeping yourself well and happy, rested and relaxed is really beneficial. Get outside in nature, turn the phone off and breathe in the fresh air and the goodness given off by the plants and trees. This is good for us and gives us our 'happy hormones' which will be passed on to the baby.

How to tap with a toddler

You can introduce your toddler to tapping by showing them as you do it yourself. Explain that you do it so you feel better when things go wrong, when you feel upset or cross or when you feel tired and can't get to sleep or if you see something scary.

Show them that feelings live in their body by helping them with this exercise.

Print off this picture of a child or draw your own. You could even draw round your child.

Give them some coloured pencils and ask them what feeling words they know, although you will probably know what they are, it's good to know which ones come to mind for them. As they mention a feeling, ask them what colour that feeling would be and where in the body it lives. Then they can colour that in on the outline.

Do this for each feeling so you have different colours in the body.

Explain that the bad feelings can be tapped away when we tap on certain points in the body, and that this connects to where they've coloured in.

Now may be the chance to show them the tapping points on the picture below.

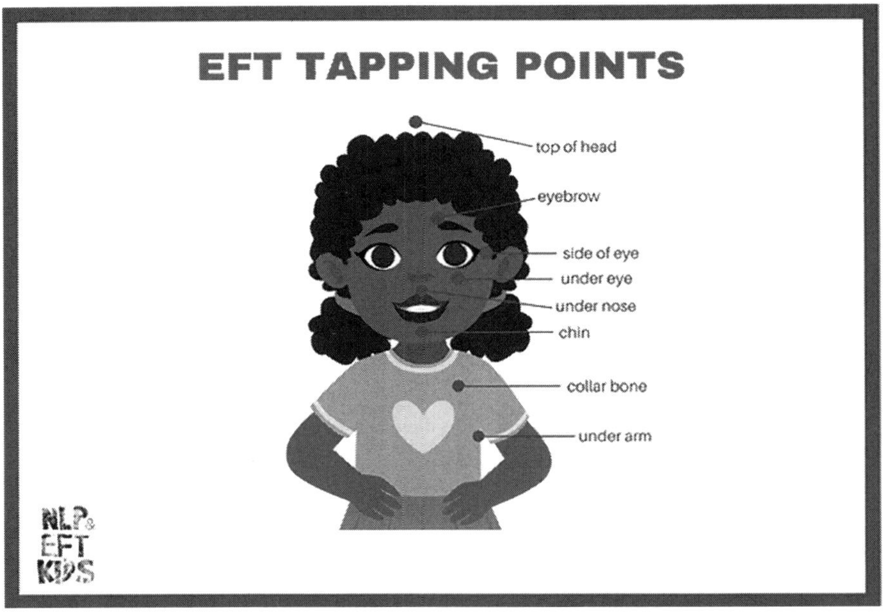

Maybe they'd like to have a go?

What bad feeling would they like to get rid of?

Can they point to it on their picture?

You can tap together, so start with a set-up on the karate-chop point and ask them to say it after you.

> "Even though I feel (feeling) and it's in my (part of the body) and it's (colour) I am a good boy/girl."

Do this three times.

Now tap round the points, showing them where to tap, using the diagram and touching the points with their finger. Tap with them so they can see where to tap and tap 6-7 times gently on each point as you both say the name of the feeling, the colour and where it is in the body.

They will soon notice that the feeling has gone. It moves fast in children.

This is a good opportunity to ask them whether there are any times when they could use this new magic tapping, such as when they have trouble settling at night or feel scared of the dark, get cross or upset and so on. Maybe introduce daily tapping with them.

Parenting toddlers can be very confusing and challenging, tiring and frustrating so make sure you tap on yourself to keep calm.

> "Even though I haven't a clue what he/she wants I love and accept myself anyway."

> "Even though I'm really tired, I am a good mummy/daddy and this will soon pass."

> "Even though I'm finding this very challenging, I love him/her and I'm a good mummy/daddy, this is just a stage and it will soon pass."

It's good to also add in the feeling and the colour for your own tapping. The feeling is particularly important because it relates to what you're making this situation mean. In other words, they are simply being toddlers. Are you distorting this to mean that you are a bad mummy or daddy?

> "Even though I'm making this mean I'm a bad mummy/daddy I love and accept myself anyway."
>
> "Even though I feel a failure and it's (colour) and I feel it in my (part of the body) I love and accept myself anyway."
>
> "Even though I feel angry / useless / overwhelmed when he/she does this, and it's (colour) in my (part of the body) I love and accept myself anyway."

Global tapping

Firstly, let's talk about clearing overwhelm. This is a very common feeling for parents of children of all ages but particularly when children have difficulty expressing their feelings and their needs. This is why it's so important to encourage them to tap when they are young so they can release their own feelings rather than allowing them to build up such that they become overwhelming.

When this does happen you can help them. The beauty of tapping is that you don't need to know what you're tapping on.

Just ask them to tell you where they feel the overwhelm (or whatever word they use) and what colour it is. It's helpful too to get a SUDs level (subjective unit of distress) so you know how it's reducing as you tap together. Once you've helped them a few times, they'll be able to do it on their own which will mean they can keep these feelings at bay so they don't build up. It's a great way for them to build confidence, knowing they can manage these feelings.

The set-up will be something like this:

> "Even though I feel overwhelmed and it's in my (part of the body) and it's (colour) I love and accept myself anyway."
>
> "Even though I feel overwhelmed / I don't know what I feel/ it is (colour) and it's in my (part of the body) and I am a good boy/girl."
>
> "Even though it all feels too much for me to cope with and it's (colour) in my (part of the body) I'll soon be OK and I'm a good boy/girl."

Tap round the body using the usual points or round the fingers, and say the words they are using even if you just keep repeating the word 'overwhelmed' and say the colour and part of the body.

The overwhelmed feeling will reduce and may be replaced by a more specific feeling and if this happens you can repeat the set-up with the new feeling and tap on that. You may find yourself doing several set-ups with them as they chunk down to the core feeling at the heart of the overwhelm. Be patient and keep going so you can clear it all by breaking it down into the 'aspects' that have contributed to the overwhelm.

When they don't know

Children sometimes don't know what the problem is and sometimes this will be true for us, too.

We can help them using tapping even in these situations. You can, however, use a few questions first to see if you can help them identify the issues.

Here are a few ideas:

"When will you know?"

"When did you know?"

"If you did know, what would it be?"

"Who knows?"

The reason we ask these questions is because they may know but be reluctant to tell us.

These questions are examples of 'clean questions' because we aren't suggesting anything, simply being curious.

It also assumes that the reason can be known to someone, so therefore it isn't a complete mystery. By suggesting someone might know, it opens the door as it were for them to also be curious and think what it could be. Then of course you can move on to the specific chapter in Part 2.

If they still don't know, that's fine, it happens a lot. Just set-up with that but ask them to tune in first because sometimes just the act of tuning in, being still and connecting with that 'I don't know' feeling, can bring something up. It might be a response to not knowing such as frustration, anger or confusion and we can tap on that. Go to the relevant chapter in part 2.

If nothing else comes up and they still don't know we can tap on 'I don't know'.

> "Even though I don't know what I feel, and it's (colour) and in my (part of the body) I am a good boy/girl."

> "Even though I wish I knew but I don't know, that's Ok for now."

> "Even though I have this feeling and I don't know what it is, it is (colour) and it's in my (part of the body)"

Give it a SUDs level so you know what's happening and can tell when it's much reduced.

Now start the tapping rounds just saying 'I don't know' and the colour and the part of the body. Do two rounds and check back in at the karate chop point where you did the set-up to see what's come up, if anything. If at this point they do know then head off to the relevant chapter in Part 2. If they don't then continue tapping but first do a 9-step gamut.

Find the groove on the hand between the little finger and the ring finger of your non-dominant hand. Use the index and middle finger of your dominant hand to tap gently on that groove. As you do this you need to also:

- Open eyes
- Close eyes
- Drop eye gaze down to your left
- Drop eye gaze down to your right
- Circle eyes clockwise
- Circle eyes anticlockwise

- Hum a tune
- Count to 9
- Hum a tune

This may shift something so you may be ready to tap on something specific. If that's the case, go to the relevant chapter in Part 2.

In Part 2 you will find the chapters on specific issues. Look up the one closest to what you feel your child is experiencing and if there doesn't seem to be one, use a global issue tapping to start with. Tap on 'how I feel' or whatever words they use. You can even tap on 'I don't know how I feel'. Then as a specific issue comes up you can refer to that chapter and read it before doing the next tapping with them.

Daily wellness habits

A major change that I've noticed since I wrote *Be a happier parent with NLP* is how much more aware we are now of the mental health of our children. Mindfulness has been introduced into schools and has been part of the curriculum for some years and, gradually, tapping has also been introduced. Schools take mental health seriously and provide counselling services, acknowledging that children need emotional and mental support alongside their educational needs.

As parents, we too are watching our children for signs that all might not be well. I would caution, though, that children know this and have noticed that they get more attention when they say they feel sad than when they say they're happy.

I've also noticed that where, in the past, it would be parents wanting their child to come and see me, nowadays it is likely to be the child who asks for help. They are much more aware of when they need help and are willing to ask for it. Children speak a different language now and openly talk about anger issues, anxiety and low self-esteem in a way that would have been quite unusual ten years ago.

Essential oils are quite commonplace in households, as are diffusers in children's bedrooms and oils being used for minor first aid. Crystals are not used as widely as oils yet, but as parents talk about them, they are starting to be used by teenagers, I notice.

Yoga, which used to be just something a parent does and was still considered a bit 'out there', is now very well-known and baby and children's yoga is widely available. There are many yoga apps so even people who would be shy about going to a class, or who have work and family commitments making it difficult to find time for a class, can do it in the privacy of their home.

Writing journals, 'morning pages', gratitude diaries and other similar ways to express thoughts and feelings so they don't build up, are also becoming popular and journaling finds its way into most wellness articles these days.

I'm going to take you through some of these and suggest how you might incorporate them into your parenting. Some you may be more drawn to than others of course but the map is not the territory; your child may embrace something that doesn't appeal to you. Remember, too, that they may dismiss an idea one day and then a few weeks later when a friend mentions it or an influencer they follow on Instagram talks about it, suddenly your idea is more interesting.

Let's start with **journaling**.

This isn't keeping a diary or writing what you need to get done, like homework, or things you need to remember to take to school like PE kit. Journaling is more a stream of consciousness. The idea behind it is that when we brush our feelings under the rug, pretend they don't exist, they don't matter, what you are saying is, "I don't matter".

We suppress our needs and emotions and this creates a biological effect of increasing the stress hormones in our body, making us more vulnerable to illness. I think it's widely known that people in stressful jobs that they don't like, tend to take more sick days off than people who may be just as busy, but like what they do. Similarly, a child who is happy at school wants to go in and will tend to be healthier than one who doesn't.

The idea, then, of journaling is to spend some time, every day, pouring out thoughts and feelings and clearing them from the mind. The writing is not to be read, certainly not by parents and often not by the writer, because it isn't about the writing at all, it's just about getting it out of the mind and onto a page.

Of course, many children do write the good stuff too and this can be done in the same place or some use a 'gratitude journal' for this as a special place to read the entries and feel happy. I have clients who like to doodle in their journals or stick things in it.

I encourage children to use this writing opportunity at the end of the day to do a feedback sandwich; writing what went well that day, what they hope will be better tomorrow and overall what they are grateful for. This really helps them to have closure on the day rather than worrying about it and not being able to sleep.

You may get some resistance at first but even if they start off by just writing a few words each day, I've heard from parents that when they get in the habit of it, they find it helpful. You might, too!

Meditation is another good way to finish the day and promote a peaceful night's sleep. It's something lots of parents and children do together as a family meditation habit. Just a short meditation every day can finish the day off calmly and quietly. Most of the meditations on phone apps have gentle calming background music, some have themes such as sleep, anxiety, relationships and others are more general.

I've seen on YouTube that there are meditations specifically for the toddlers and little ones as well.

I love the Ho'oponopono meditation. It is believed to be a simple and powerful way to heal relationships while also healing ourselves. It originated in Hawaii as an ancient healing method based on forgiveness. Within families we can have quite intense situations and forgiveness seems a bigger word than just a muttered 'sorry'. There are Ho'oponopono meditations and books you can buy if this interests you.

The words are:

I love you
I'm sorry
Please forgive me
Thank you

Most parents are familiar with **mindfulness** and its concepts, but I wonder whether it gets a bit confused with meditation.

Mindfulness is about paying attention in the present moment to whatever is happening right now, without judgement, and without the need to fix, react or do anything at all, rather to just be there in the moment with what 'is'.

> "Paying attention in the present moment on purpose, non-judgmentally." Jan Kabat Zin

I did my mindfulness training when my youngest was about 10-12 years old, transitioning to secondary school, and I remember the hardest part of mindfulness for me was that 'non-judgmental' bit. Actually, being still and doing nothing was also pretty challenging. I don't know how the kids do it.

The focus is on the breath, the idea being to just focus on breathing in and out and when you get distracted, to be aware of the distraction but to let it go and come back to the breath. My trainer used to tell us when we get distracted, imagine gently guiding our attention back to the breath as if it were a small child who has strayed too far from your side. I love that analogy.

I don't use that with the children I work with. Instead, I ask them to imagine being on a railway platform waiting for a train. The train they want is the happiness train that will take them somewhere nice and fun, maybe a theme park. A train arrives and on the front it says 'worrying about exams' and this is their usual train so they are tempted to get on it. But wait, think about where that train will go. It won't go anywhere good and it will end up back at the same station. So let the train doors close and let that train leave without you. Then another train arrives. This one is going to 'worrying what my friends are saying about me'. This train is also familiar. But again, it won't go anywhere and will just come back to the same old platform. Let it pass and wait for the train going somewhere you want to go.

Children find this helpful, they know that the same thoughts keep reoccurring and don't get them anywhere and yet they still attach themselves to those thoughts. The idea of simply noting the unhelpful thoughts and coming back to the breath with no judgement appeals to them as a new way to be calm and resourced.

Instead of focusing on what happened that day and looking back to what has already been (the past) or worrying about what tomorrow will bring (the future) being in the present gives them peace. Children cannot control the past or the future, but they can control the present.

Practising mindfulness promotes skills controlled by the prefrontal cortex such as focus and cognitive control which helps children build patience and concentration. It has to be practised, though, and the best person to help them with this is you.

Here are a few mindfulness exercises to do with your children. Let's start with the raisin eating one.

Mindful eating exercise

- Take a raisin or other small fruit object that you have to hand and put it in your child's palm.
- Ask them to imagine they have arrived from Mars and have never seen anything like this before. What on earth is it?
- Use all their senses to explore it.
- Look at it from every angle.
- Notice the colour, is it the same colour all the way round.
- Look at its shape and size.
- Look at its texture.
- Turn it around in their hand.
- How does it feel?
- What about its weight?
- Does the surface feel soft and smooth, or rough?
- How dense is it? Can they squeeze it?
- Now listen. Does it make any noise?
- Is there a smell?
- What does it remind them of?
- Now take it to your mouth and put it against your lips.
- What is the feel on the lips?

- Is there taste on the lips?
- Put it on the tongue.
- First at the front,
- Then middle,
- Then back.
- Where is the taste strongest?
- Try each side of the mouth.
- Does one side taste more than the other?
- Imagine where it has grown.
- Who has cultivated it? What are they like? Where do they live?
- How did it get to your house?
- How many different people were involved in the process of getting it from the plant to your mouth?
- Now bite on it.
- Where do you feel the taste sensation?
- Where in the mouth?
- Do you feel it in the throat?
- Now swallow it and notice the taste as it passes down your throat and as you swallow.

This is an example of how we do a thing mindfully, taking time to notice every sensation as it happens and paying attention to it 100%.

You can do this as you walk, take a shower, brush your teeth. Take something you do every day and do it mindfully for a week, noticing how this feels calming and nurturing.

It is a good idea to develop healthy wellness routines with your children that will set them up for life. Increasingly, we appreciate that our mental health affects everything we do at school, work, home and in our community. How can we concentrate at school if we haven't slept? How can we enjoy our sport if we haven't eaten well? We will have no energy. Our mind and body are connected. How we treat our body will impact our thinking and ability to process our world. How we think will affect how we move.

The fastest way to change our state of mind is through our physiology. Laughter, exercise, and movement will bring our energy and concentration levels up as the energy shifts around the body, bringing us more into flow. Yoga, deep breathing, meditation and mindfulness will slow down that busy chattering mind and allow us to de-stress and relax.

You can help your children at various times during the day to create the best state for whatever they are about to do.

In the morning they need to be alert, focused and ready to learn so some activity will help. Joe Wicks knew what he was doing by setting kids up first thing with his popular PE routine.

Again, after lunch children need another energy shift so they can concentrate on their afternoon lessons, so running around at lunch break will help, as will not having too much carbohydrate in packed lunches, having instead plenty of protein and food that releases its energy slowly.

Children need another boost of energy to do their homework so getting the chance to run around the garden or the park before sitting down again to work would be helpful, plus another snack. But then they need to wind down before bed and be able to settle feeling relaxed, positive and with an empty mind, free of stress and worry.

For this stage of the day, mindfulness, meditation, journaling, a gratitude diary are all great options. The idea is to empty any stresses or worries out of the mind and onto the page or into an app. There's a lovely one I use called 'Morning pages' which encourages you to write 250 words a day straight into your phone and it feels like you've dumped it in the phone and out of your mind.

However well you support your child's wellbeing, there will be days when they don't want to go into school, times when they don't want to do their homework or feel they can't and problems getting them to bed or to sleep.

For those times I would recommend tapping, as a family wellness tool that any of you can use to help each other. There will be times you may appreciate them noticing that you need a bit of support, too. This is how schools find that it works. Tapping becomes the automatic 'go to' when someone needs a bit of extra support.

PART 2

Introduction

This section of the book is written so you can go to whichever chapter you need at the time. Because of this, I've had to repeat explanations of different techniques although of course they will be slightly different depending on the issue you're reading about.

If you've come straight to this section and are wondering where to find issues such as 'overwhelm' or simply not knowing what's wrong, these are covered in Part 1 as they are what we call 'global issues'.

You will find that issues and situations can have a number of aspects with different emotions and that emotions change as you work on them. I've tried to cover this in each section but start by asking your child; "what would you call what you're feeling right now?" Another way is to guess and wonder what you'd be feeling if you were displaying similar behaviour.

1. Anger
2. Anxiety
3. Coping with change
4. Fear of failure
5. Fears and Phobias
6. Friendship
7. Learning struggles
8. Low self-esteem
9. Sleep

1

Anger

Children use words like 'mad', 'lost it', 'cross', 'explode' to describe this feeling so use this chapter for whatever word your family uses. Many parents talk about 'melt down'. I will be using the word 'anger' throughout to keep it consistent.

I like to describe the anger response as being like the prickles of a hedgehog, sharp and painful but ultimately there to protect the soft underbelly of the hedgehog, to protect its vulnerability. Unless it puts out its prickles, it will die. This need to protect themselves is one that children very much relate to. They don't set out to attack. Anger is a response. It's important to remember this and seek to discover the trigger.

The natural response of most parents is to ask, "Why are you angry?" or "What happened?" We want to know how we can help, how we fix this. What was the 'trigger'? we want to know. Your child will possibly tell you what just happened to cause them to show their prickles but there is a whole sequence of events before this that we need to understand.

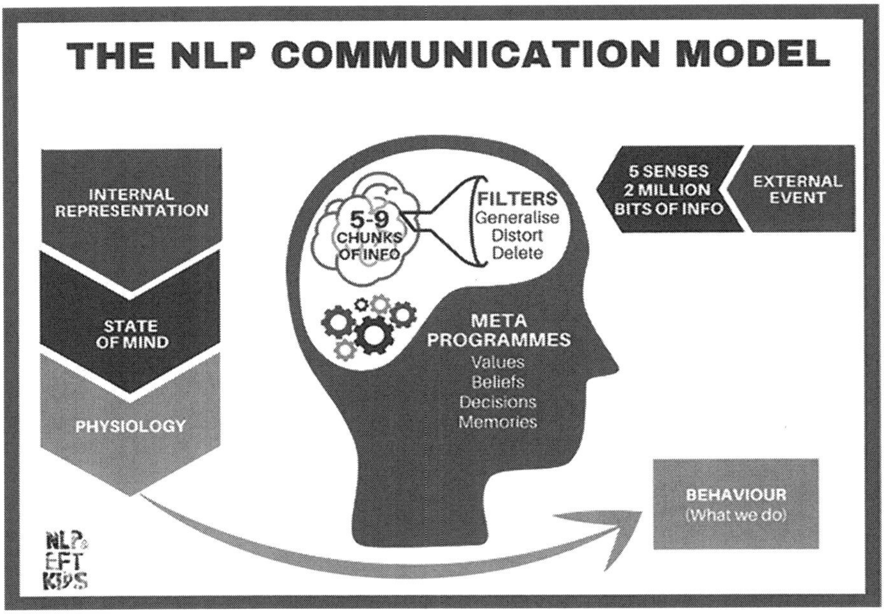

A 'trigger' can be a number of things that all happen in a moment.

- Someone does or says something and we call this an 'external event'
- We filter it through our
  - Beliefs
  - Values
  - Experiences
  - Way of processing our world (our VAK and metaprogrammes)
  - Memories
- This gives us an internal representation of the event – what we make it mean
- This creates a 'state' or mood, attitude, feeling
- This shows in our body, our physiology
- Then there is a behaviour - in this case, an angry response
- And that is the next 'external event' and so it keeps circling and evolving

What we as parents need to do is work on the filters so that our child creates a different internal representation. This is what I do when I'm working with clients by understanding these beliefs, values, experiences and memories so I can help them re-frame them into a new, more resourceful belief, that will create a different internal representation.

A good first step I think is to think about your own anger. Your child is 'of you'. They have been modelling you since the day they were born, even before.

This exercise is called the Anger Onion.

Exercise

Think of a time when you felt angry. If it helps, put your hand to your heart, close your eyes and look down. This enables you to sink within and block out your conscious mind which may be making excuses, giving explanations and causes such as 'but he/she did......' which will, I think, remind you that anger is a response.

Now complete this sentence:

"I felt angry when..."

Try to focus on observable behaviour rather than jumping ahead to what you think their intention was or what you assumed. For example:

> "I felt angry when Ben deliberately pushed Annie on the floor and hurt her arm."

Imagine you are a CCTV camera and what it sees. This is called 'disassociating' and it takes our parental assumptions out and just sees what actually happened. This then becomes:

> "I felt angry when I saw Ben push Annie and it looked as if she hurt her arm."

You have now removed your assumptions. My experience of children is that the 'hurt' child will definitely play it up to get their sibling into trouble and clients I've talked to, have told me that their children do this.

Now, on to the next stage:

> "I felt hurt because.."

Acknowledge the hurt behind your anger. You may need to go back and tune in again to the feelings you had at that time.

There could be all sorts of reasons for your hurt. Here are a few guesses:

- I wasn't in the room at the time, felt guilty and responsible
- I was on the phone/working/busy and didn't see what happened
- I'd already spoken to Ben about his behaviour and thought he'd understood
- He always does this just before going to school and we'll be late again
- It's my fault because we got divorced/moved/changed schools
- I don't understand why he gets so angry
- It's my fault because I shouted at him earlier

As you will see, lots of these hurts are about us. We have made his behaviour mean something about ourselves and we have in some way, taken responsibility and made it about us rather than trying to understand what was going on for them.

Now the next step is:

> "What I needed (but didn't get) was for............................"

This is about us meeting our own needs and we will talk about that when I tell you about the Drama Triangle.

What was your need in the moment just before you became angry?

Again, my guesses would be

- To be heard
- To be seen
- To be listened to
- To be obeyed
- For your needs to be met
- To feel supported
- To not be so busy

This is likely to be very specific for you, so write in your own needs at that moment.

Finally, the last and most important part,

> "What I feared was.."

This is the nitty gritty of it, that soft underbelly, the fear.

For a child, the answers tend to be:

- That mummy loves him/her more than me
- That I don't matter
- That I'm stupid
- That I'm not important
- That he/she has more than me
- That he/she doesn't like me
- That he/she wants to get me in trouble
- That it will be my fault
- That I'll be punished

For you? I'm guessing these may be likely answers:

- I'm a bad parent
- He /she doesn't respect me
- He /she doesn't love me
- I'm useless
- I won't get custody
- I'll be in trouble
- I can't cope
- What I say doesn't matter
- They don't listen to me
- I'm not important

A good response to these beliefs is to challenge them. These beliefs are often formed in early childhood and, without realising it, we can find ourselves attracting situations that appear to be evidence that these beliefs are actually facts. They aren't.

Think about a belief you have in times of anger.

My belief is that ....

Now write down the opposite belief, one you'd like to have instead.

I'd like to believe that ....

Now give yourself a mission to look for evidence of where that is true for you.

What we focus on is what we get more of.

I find when children do this anger onion exercise it is a real moment of understanding. They had no idea what their anger was about and tended to focus on what had just happened before. Now they know that it wasn't the event but what they made it mean, it was their fear and vulnerability. This insight enabled them to treat themselves with some gentleness and forgiveness rather than being angry at their angry reaction. By making sense of it, they could manage it better, understand next time it happens and know how to look at it from another angle, reframe it.

This leads on to **EFT**. With or without the understanding of the fear or need behind the anger, we can teach children to manage anger with tapping.

EFT Tapping script for anger

Here's a tapping script you can use. The script is to teach them how to use it for their anger, assuming they are not actually feeling angry at that moment because if they are, it isn't necessarily a good teaching opportunity!

Step 1

Ask them to think about a time when they felt angry, cross, frustrated or whatever word they tend to use. Lots of children use the word 'mad' for anger. It helps if they close their eyes and put their hands to their chest, breathing in for four and out for four, three times.

> "As you think about this time when you felt angry (or their word) where in your body do you feel it?"

"What colour is that angry feeling?"

"What size is it?" (use fruit as a measure i.e. grape, apple, melon)

"Is it moving or still?"

"Is it solid or more liquid, like a...?"

"On a scale of 0–10 with 10 being the worst and zero being no anger at all, what score would you give that angry feeling?"

This is called the 'SUDs level, meaning subjective unit of distress.

Of course, they are tuning into the memory of it so if you're doing this when they are very angry, the score will be much higher but as I've said, it would be better to separate the teaching from the healing.

I think it's also fun to use metaphor, especially with children.

"If your anger was an animal, what animal would it be?"

I might continue this by asking:

"What does your animal want?"

Using metaphors is a gentler way of working with children because it is very much their language and they can project their own thoughts and feelings onto the animal they've chosen without having to own the feelings themselves. So maybe they might say "my dragon says no one is listening to him and it makes him feel mad and want to breathe fire over them".

Step 2 – The set-up

Now we are ready to start the tapping. Ask your child to put out their non-dominant hand as if they were doing a karate chop and use their dominant hand to tap lightly on the side of their other hand on that soft place between the base of the little finger and the wrist.

You say the words first and they repeat after you, we say it three times, varying a little each time.

> "Even though I have this (word they use for angry) feeling in my (part of the body) I am a good boy/girl."

> "Even though I have this (colour) (feeling) in my (part of the body) I am a good boy/girl."

> "Even though I have this angry dragon (use their words of course) in my (part of the body) I am a good boy/girl."

The idea here is to acknowledge that it is OK to feel angry sometimes but it doesn't mean they are defined by their anger, they are still a good boy or girl.

Sometimes I find children already feel a bit calmer having done this set-up. This can be because the side of the hand tapping point connects to the central nervous system.

Step 3 – Tapping rounds

Now we are ready to show them how to tap around the body on the meridian tapping points.

Starting with the top of the head, we use the flat of the hand to tap as we say a reminder phrase. The words we use here will be the child's words. So tapping in this order:

Top of the head
Eyebrow point
Side of the eye
Under the eye
Under the nose
Under the mouth

Collarbone
Under the arm

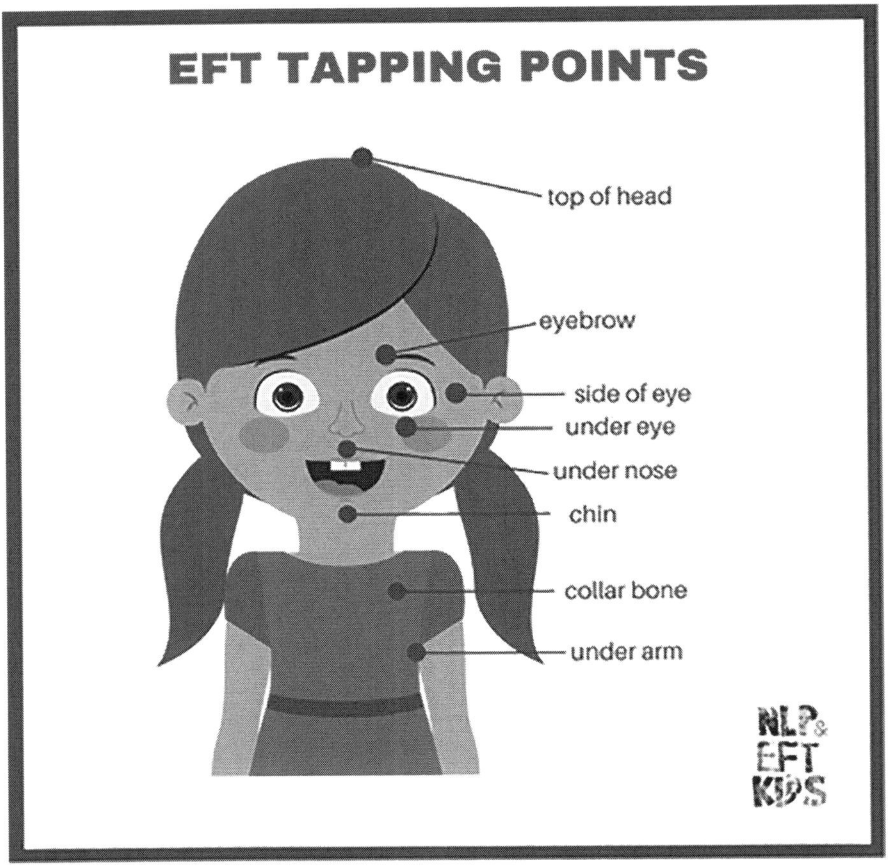

The words will be the colour, the part of the body, the feeling and any other words they use. So if for example they say they have red anger in their tummy and it is the size of an apple, spiky and moving about, you would use any of these words as you tap around the body.

Do two complete rounds of tapping and ask your child how they feel. Check in with them whether there have been changes in the intensity (the SUDs level of 0-10) and check the colour because that can change along with the part of the body. Ask about the feeling, too. It's not unusual for anger to turn to sadness. For example, say if your child has been told off at school for something he didn't do, he will come home angry as he tells you about it. At the time, he may have felt sad at being picked on. Once he's expressed his anger about it, he may then feel sad again.

Using the new updated information continue to tap on the same tapping points but with the new colour, emotion, part of the body and size. We're looking for the SUDs level to drop to around 3 or 4.

Keep tapping and you could encourage your child to breathe and move to tapping on the finger points which mean using the thumb and first finger of the dominant hand to gently squeeze the top of each finger of the other hand around the nail. This works well for school as they can tap under their desk if they need to.

Once the SUDs level is down to zero or 1, or when your child says they feel much better, you can stop.

I like to use **Perceptual Positioning** for anger and I think your child will as well. The reason it appeals to children is because their anger can sometimes seem like an alien or a part of themselves they barely recognise. Being able to separate it and place it on a chair, talk to it and try to understand it, can be an empowering exercise.

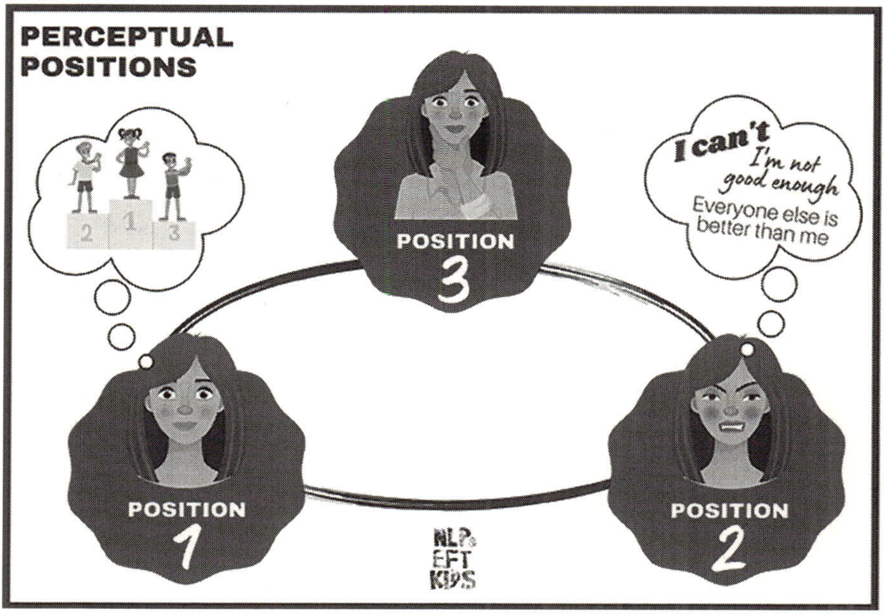

Set out three chairs in a triangle and ask them to choose one for themselves. That is the 'I' chair. It's where they will sit and speak from their own viewpoint. The exercise is called Perceptual Positioning because it invites the child to experience the situation from three different perspectives: I, You and Them.

'You' is the part of them that they are working on so this could be their limiting belief, it could be someone they have had conflict with, it could be a situation or feeling, in this case, anger. In this exercise they get the chance to 'be' this part of themselves and understand its motivation, positive intention and what it needs from them in order to be reassured. That part of us that stops us from getting what we want, being who we want to be, has a positive intention and once that's understood, it will be under control rather than controlling us.

'Them' is the impartial bystander that we go to at the end to get that unemotional observation of the two sides of us in order to get a disassociated perspective.

Step 1

Sitting in the 'I' chair they speak to their anger sitting in the 'You' chair.

What would they like to say to their anger?

They should address their anger as if it is separate from them. Some children like me to put a monkey or stuffed toy in that chair so they feel as if they are talking to a 'thing' rather than just an empty chair.

When they've said something, and it doesn't matter what they say as there are no right or wrong things to say to 'anger', they stand up.

Step 2

Break state. This means having a bit of a shimmy and a shake. The reason for this is to check out of one state of being - 'I' - before stepping into the state of being 'you', the anger. If we don't do that, the child may forget who they are. We need to distinguish clearly between the two positions or perceptions.

Step 3

Ask your child to sit in Position 2, the 'you' or in this case 'anger' chair. Here they need to' associate into that anger. That means that they imagine it as if it's happening right now. What's it like to be the anger? How do they feel about Position 1? What is making them angry?

Step 4

Break state again.

Step 5

Your child goes back to Position 1 and back to being himself. He needs to respond to what the anger has said. How does he feel about it?

Basically, what happens is that your child needs to alternately be himself and his anger until there is some understanding. Ideally your child needs to understand what positive intention his anger has for him.

Once he knows, he can then decide how he can control it.

This exercise tends to lead to a good resolution for the child and better understanding of how to change their thoughts for more resourceful ones.

Step 6

We finish the exercise by sitting in chair 3, the 'impartial bystander' chair and commenting on what they've noticed and what they now understand about the situation.

This is an opportunity to have a chat with your child as to what small step they could make towards a different way of behaving. Who in your family is good at controlling their anger?

One of the aspects of NLP that make it different from other therapies is the belief that we can acquire other people's models of excellence when we copy them. We do this in several ways:

- Observe the structure of what they do
- Listen to the language pattern
- Extract their belief about this

Modelling exercise

Invite whoever in the family they have identified as a model of excellence for being calm in an argument or able to control their anger to be the model. You may need to have a chat about what specifically they'd like to model because it is important to model what they'd like to be like.

When they know, complete this sentence.

> I'd like to model the way .... is able to ....

Now ask them.

What you need to find out is their belief about staying calm. Why is it important to them? How do they do it? When you have an answer, write it below.

> The belief I need is this ....

Now where in your child's life do they have this belief?

Remember from Part 1, the beliefs of excellence, one of the NLP beliefs is that 'we already have all the resources we need'. Your child doesn't get angry in every situation. Are they able to contain it in their sport, at school, with their friends? They do have this ability.

> I have this belief in my .... where I believe ....

We can anchor this for them.

Anchoring is when we create a little reminder action to make us pause and do something different in the situation that would normally trigger us. You might suggest a little tap on the gamut point (the groove between the little finger and the ring finger). They can then do this when they are either in a situation where they might feel triggered usually or when they feel the first angry feelings and want to calm down.

Once they've used their anchor, they can breathe in for four and out for four to settle their breath which will also serve to calm their state.

A final exercise to help with anger is the **Drama Triangle**.

Stephen Karpman developed the Drama Triangle around the same time as NLP to explain the dynamic created when someone decides to play 'victim'.

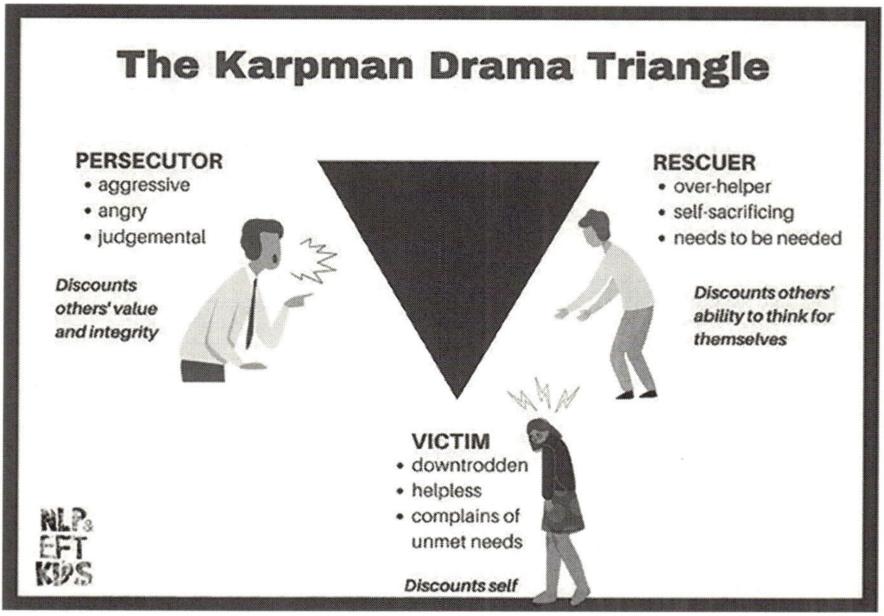

'Victim' is the 'poor me' position, where your child initially feels helpless, hopeless, unable to solve his problem.

The person or situation he blames for this is 'the persecutor' so the example I often give children is the story of Cinderella or indeed any number of fairy stories. Cinderella of course is the 'Victim', as she can't go to the ball. She blames the ugly stepsisters so they are the 'Persecutors'. The 'Rescuer' is then the fairy godmother who fixes the problem.

Persecutors typically shout a lot and get angry and feel they are not being heard. It is never their fault. They get angry.

The Rescuer steps in to help the Victim by fixing the problem. Victim and Rescuer often develop a co-dependent relationship and many families see this with the mother taking the Rescuer role to a child in the family.

But this is a dynamic. It is not a static situation and we're here to explore anger.

Let's say child A is quietly doing their homework in their bedroom. Child B comes in and annoys them, takes their phone perhaps. Child A asks for it back but child B runs off with it. So Child A feel like the victim and to him Child B is the persecutor (the baddy). But Child A runs after child B and snatches it back, slightly hurting child B who runs to Mummy, the Rescuer. Child A is angry. He's done nothing wrong apart from trying to get his phone back so he moves to Persecutor, shouting at Mother that she should tell child B off for coming into his room and taking things. But Mummy is cross with him because he shouldn't have hurt his brother. Child A goes back to victim and child B smirks and moves to Persecutor again teasing and taunting.

This is a fairly typical Drama Triangle where Victim and sometimes Rescuer can end up as Persecutor and when a child is angry we need to understand the structure of exactly what happened and who the victim was because it is easy to blame the one appearing to be the Persecutor when in fact they were simply taking action to protect themselves, their property, their privacy or something precious to them.

So what can we do as parents?

1. Probably the first thing would be to resist the temptation to fix and be a rescuer. Step away and let them sort things out for themselves.
2. Ask what they need. We often step in and assume what's needed or who is to blame.
3. Encourage the 'victim' to come up with their own solution. That's how they step away from the triangle and become empowered and build self-esteem, not by having all their problems solved by the rescuer.
4. Allow the 'victim' to fail in the belief that this is how they learn. As parents we often protect our children but in doing so we don't prepare them for the world where failure is a daily occurrence.
5. Talk to the 'persecutor' because the reason they are shouting and blaming is because they have felt like 'victim' but no one was listening so now they have to shout.

Anger is the outward sign that needs are not being met. They are hurting but because no one is listening they have to shout louder and get more angry. No child ever wakes up thinking they will be angry today. It is not a desired state but is what happens when everything else has failed.

2

Anxiety

You would not be alone if, when your child or teen tells you they feel anxious, you ask why. This is a natural reaction. We want to know why they feel anxious so that we can reassure them. The trouble with this is that it tends to make things worse because, instead of being present with the anxiety and managing it in ways I will explain in this chapter, they reject the feeling as 'bad' or 'confusing'. They ask themselves 'why' and their brain says 'I have no idea' or 'you are stupid to be anxious' or 'don't you know, silly?' In their desire to please you and also not to feel silly, they dig around for a logical or likely reason for feeling anxious and tell you that one. This may well be more understandable to you, the parent, and it will pacify the child for a while as distraction therapy, but it won't show them how to self-soothe and manage the emotion themselves.

This results in a **Drama Triangle** where they become the victim who feels anxious and can't do something, you become the rescuer who sorts everything out for them, and the 'thing' or person who was the supposed cause of the anxiety becomes the persecutor.

Of course, in the Fairy stories I mentioned earlier everything works out in the end as the victim gets what they want, but it is always as a result of it being 'fixed' by someone else.

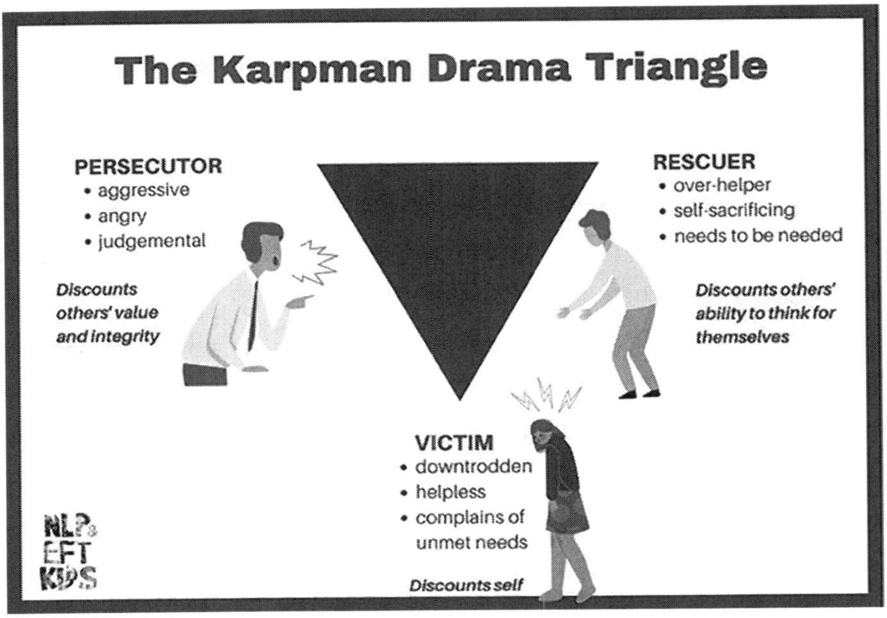

Instead, you can help them with their anxiety by using coaching techniques to encourage them to perceive the situation differently.

1. Ask them what <u>they</u> could do, what their options are in this situation. They will be inclined to look at it from a binary point of view: do it or not do it. However, what if there were more options? Having more options opens things up. In order to think of options we need to use our imagination and to create possibilities. This already makes the situation look better.
2. Remember in Part 1 you read about the NLP Metaprogrammes and one of them was big chunk/small chunk, where I described how some of us are more comfortable with concepts and others need detail? Children who are faced with a chunk size that they struggle with will feel anxious. Show them how to chunk it down by asking what specifically they are concerned about and ask how they could find the smallest first step that they can manage. Show them how to chunk up by asking how, by doing this thing, they achieve something meaningful or meet some bigger purpose.

3. Have they done something similar before? Can they imagine being able to do it in the future? I like to use a **Time Line** for this exercise.

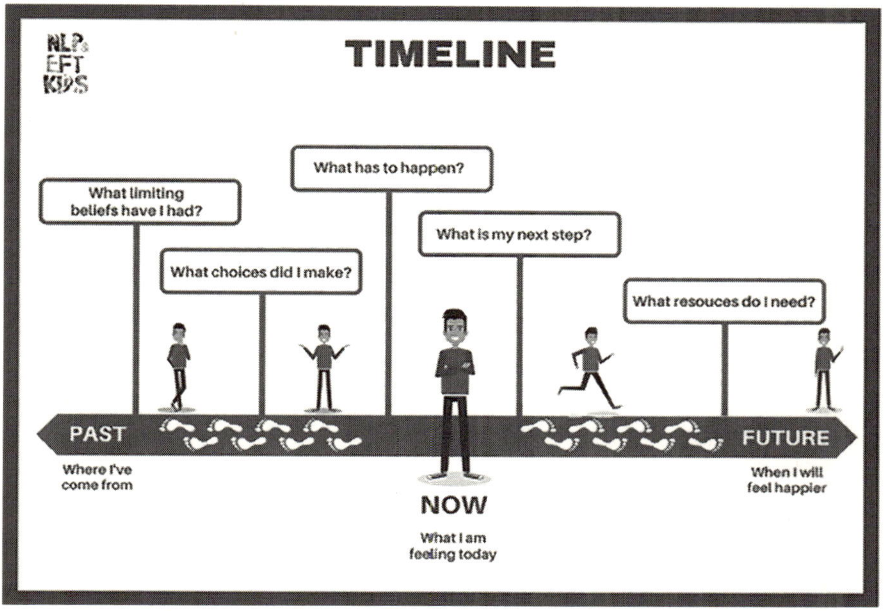

Exercise

Ask them to imagine a line along the floor. At one end is birth and the other end age 18yrs or when they leave school or university (choose an age that they will consider relevant). They should then stand on the point on the line which they feel represents today or their age now.

What do they want to do? Ask them to express it as what they want, not what they don't want. When children are anxious they tend to drop into an 'away from' thinking pattern (metaprogrammes section in Part 1) and focus on what they don't want. As you can imagine, whatever you focus on is what you get more of, it's what you attract. So expressing it as an "I want ...." is already a step in the right direction.

Now ask them to look back down the Time Line to their younger years and ask when they did something similar. Tempting though it might be to prompt them, as I'm sure you can think of just the thing, resist for as long as possible then just *suggest* rather than tell them. After all, to them it might not have been similar. The prompt might help them think of something that is.

They should go and stand on that point on the Time Line when they did that similar thing. If they absolutely can't think of anything similar, they can go into the future on their line to a time when they can or will do this thing. Wherever they are standing now, whether at a point where they've done something similar or a time when they will do this, they are on a positive point representing possibility.

On that point, they can do an **anchoring** which is when you ask them to think of something that will remind them of being able to do this thing. Ask them to imagine that state of being how they want to feel. I'm reluctant to name it because it's important you use their words. The opposite of anxious isn't obvious. I've heard children use words like 'confident' or 'brave' rather than 'relaxed' or 'calm'. Other words like 'cool' come up as well. What we don't want is for them to say 'not anxious' as their desired state as this is what we call 'away from' thinking. It is notoriously difficult to anchor a state of not being something. So, encourage them to think about the feeling they do want not what they don't want or want less of.

It could be visual (imagining themselves doing it), auditory (imagining what they'll say or what they will hear when they've done it) or kinaesthetic (what they will feel). All three will be great as we are trying to get them to associate into the act of doing this thing. I explain it like this:

> "When we feel anxious it can feel like a ship being tossed on the sea, right? You feel as if you have no control over your emotions. So imagine you have an anchor you can drop onto the sea bed to hold your ship steady so it doesn't bob about in the waves? If you had such an anchor to keep you steady, what could you do to remind yourself that you have this anchor?"

You need an easy action that your child can do at school, out with friends or anywhere. Here are some examples of anchors children I've worked with have used:

- Stroking their arm to remind themselves of stroking their pet to feel calm
- Thumbs up sign
- Putting their hand on their heart
- Tapping their chin
- Imagining their favourite place
- Saying 'you can do it!'

Ask them to think of a small action they can do to remind them of what they have just created, maybe a small tap on the wrist or a finger? It needs to be something they can do discreetly in the moment.

When they are totally immersed in the feeling they should use the action that is their anchor for the feeling. When the feeling passes, they release the anchor.

Do this three times or more so that when they use their anchor they get the feeling they want. Children have great imagination so this tends to take about 3 goes.

Now ask them to walk slowly, using the anchor, to their starting point, today's place on the Time Line. Ask them how they feel now about the thing that was making them feel anxious.

Then ask them to think about an event in the future that would normally make them feel anxious and ask them to go to that point on the Time Line with their anchor. How does that event feel now?

An additional fun thing you can do if your child has used an animal as their metaphor for the desired state (their word for not anxious) is that they can fly along the Time Line if they've chosen a bird or gallop/jump etc. and they can even fly above the Time Line and look down on themselves and see what they observe.

The great thing about using the Time Line is that it encourages children to think about possibility. By finding times on the line when they have felt brave or cool or confident, relaxed etc they realise that 'anxious' is not their identity. Anxious is not who they are. Anxious hasn't always been them and it won't always be them. Anxiety can become a 'stuck state'. Children can hear their parents talking about them as being 'anxious' or 'having anxiety' and, because children believe their parents know everything, they believe this to be who they are and can become 'the anxious child' in the family. It's hard to break away from that. So the Time Line gives them the chance to see how things change.

4. Think about where you put your attention and change it. As parents we naturally turn towards our child when they need us and we praise them when we feel they've done something well.

But what if they are more neutral, in that state where they're just about coping? Do we wait until they're not coping then rescue them? I know of parents who worry all day while their child is at school and greet them on return from school with a worried face, expecting the worst. Some even have an unconscious negative anchor.

One mum told me that the moment she picked up her car keys to go and collect her son from school, she started to imagine what a bad day he had probably had. So with a worried face she would ask, "What was your day like today?" and naturally the child will tell her what went wrong or what made them anxious because that is what the mum is indicating she wants to hear about. You can imagine that she communicated this expectation to him and he would be more likely to tell her what hadn't gone well than if she'd greeted him expecting to hear what had been good about his day.

Let me give you an example of a teenage boy who believed he was pleasing his mum by telling her how anxious he'd been at school. His parents believed he had an 'anxiety issue', gave him books on anxiety and constantly asked him about any anxiety he had experienced during the day so they could 'fix it'. The boy told me he was able to manage it for himself but felt he still needed to tell his mum as soon as she got home from work because 'she'd want to know'. His experiences had each lasted seconds but they were the focus of every conversation with his parents. It was as if 'fixing' this anxiety for their child made them feel they were being good parents.

If this is you, maybe think about using some of these exercises for yourself because how you present to your child will influence them. You are their model of excellence. If you tend to be anxious yourself yet tell them there's no need to be, this may be confusing. Perhaps you could learn to do these exercises for your own anxiety and then show them how to clear theirs. Once they notice changes in you they will be more engaged as they will see the exercises work.

It will be different for everyone just as what anxiety means for each of us is different. Do not assume that your child's anxiety is the same as your own.

As parents we do a lot of fixing and, whilst this seems natural when children are small and physically can't do everything for themselves, it doesn't make sense when they can. I ran a Montessori school when my children were small and I love the way Maria Montessori talks about how to empower even small children to take responsibility for themselves in terms of expressing their needs and looking after their environment, tidying things away, returning an exercise to the shelf it came from, tucking their chair back into the table so another child can walk past and so on. One of the core beliefs of excellence of NLP is that 'we already have all the resources' and that includes knowing what we need. That might seem unlikely but when we understand more about what happens in our body when we feel anxious, I think you'll find it easier to help your child.

This is how I explain anxiety to children:

> "The smoke alarm goes off – it's scary and loud – you panic, you can't move, you don't know what to do. But then you realise that it's just the toast. You've just burned the toast. No need to panic."

This is how the amygdala works. There's a small part of the brain that sends out an alarm if you are in danger, it's to protect you and keep you safe. But sometimes it overreacts and it sets off the alarm when nothing much is happening. We need to recognise those times when there really is danger and when it's just a false alarm. But in the moment of panic this is hard to do.

Another thing about anxiety is that it is rarely the event or person that is making your child feel anxious. It is what it makes them feel. Let me explain.

Something happens, something they see, hear or something done to them. They experience something. Let's say the teacher says "Class, today we are going to have a test."

Their brain filters it in three ways.

- **Deletes** – focuses only on the scared anxious feelings
- **Generalises** – makes up a rule to simplify e.g. "I'm always anxious"
- **Distorts** – foretells the future or makes an assumption – "I will be anxious"

They have now already programmed their mind to create the anxiety they expect. A way you can respond to these filters is to challenge them using what we call 'clean language'. It's tempting to reassure them, remind them that they will be fine. This, however, is to put our own assumptions onto what they've said. Instead we can repeat some of their words in a questioning manner.

When they use vague words or are not specific, such as using the word 'test', we can ask, 'What is there specifically about this test that worries you?'

When they say they are 'always anxious', we can respond, 'Always?' which prompts them to consider the times when they've been more relaxed. When it comes from them rather than us, it is more likely to be effective.

When they mindread saying what will happen, we can say, 'How do you know this?' or 'What evidence do you have?'.

Memories

Memory can be quite selective. Maybe your child has remembered a test in which they really panicked yet usually they manage well. They may be focusing on that bad experience. Reminding them that memory can play tricks like this may help. Instead of telling them when they have been calm, you could say "I'm wondering if you can think of a test where you felt quite calm and relaxed?" This again prompts them into a positive search in their memory bank.

Vision board

Get some magazines and ask them to cut out pictures, words, colours and anything that makes them feel calm and relaxed. Stick them on a sheet of paper and, if you can, laminate it and put it up on their bedroom wall so they can look at it when they need to feel calm. If your child has a smartphone they can put it on their home screen so they see it whenever they turn their phone on.

You can extend this by suggesting they notice what colours or themes they've used. If they look at it intently then close their eyes and put their hands over it, imagining that they are drawing those colours and themes into themselves, at the same time saying an affirmation such as:

- I am calm
- I am peaceful
- I am strong
- I matter

Or whatever you and your child feel will be good affirmations for this moment.

Circle of excellence

I like this exercise because it's similar to anchoring but adds another dimension: more skills.

Ask your child to think about the thing they feel anxious about.
Then ask them how they would like to feel instead.
Now get out felt pens and paper and ask them to list all the skills they have to enable them to feel as they want to feel.

Skills are things they do well. It could include qualities they have such as patience, determination, positivity, memory, imagination and so on.

When you have a list, your child will be feeling a lot more positive already, and you can ask them to imagine a circle in front of them.

You're going to say, "1, 2, 3, go!" and they will step into this imaginary circle. In the circle are all their skills from the list. They are to imagine bending down and pulling up a bubble around themselves in which all these skills exist. They hold the bubble around themselves, feeling and enjoying all the skills they have that enable them to feel good about the thing they are working with.

Now ask them to step out and we do this exercise three times. Remind them to really focus on these skills, see themselves with these skills and make the feelings stronger and more intense each time.

Then step away from the circle, they can now bend down and scoop up the circle using their thumb and index finger like a circle. I then suggest they put this in their pocket like a portable circle of excellence.

Do you see how this works as an anchor as well?

Parts Integration

You know how sometimes we feel two conflicting emotions at the same time? We can be excited about something new, perhaps, but at the same time, a bit scared. We can be looking forward to a party but worried we won't find someone nice to talk to. These two emotions exist in our mind alongside each other and can act like a see-saw, with one side up and one side down. Imagine that these parts can talk to each other. This is what we do in this exercise.

First we need to identify the two parts. You can explain the concept to your child and ask them if they have two people in their head like that, or two voices: one that wants to do something and the other that is scared or worried or anxious.

Ask your child to hold out both hands in front of them palms up.

In one hand is one thought and in the other hand, the other thought. Some children like to imagine them as animals or birds, colours, shapes, dinosaurs etc. The important thing is for them to achieve the objectivity of holding each part out in their hands so they can be disassociated and look at each voice or thought from a safe place where the emotion is on their hands not in their own body. It's often easier to understand our emotions like that when we see them at a slight distance.

So, in one hand is the part that wants something (our desirable outcome or goal or intention) and in the other hand is that thing that's stopping us, our anxiety or limiting belief about our ability to do this thing.

We are now going to have a conversation with each hand. Yes it does sound daft but I find children have so much imagination and they find this quite easy to do. As they are both parts of the same child, intuitively they know how to do this. They can do it silently or out loud.

It is one of the core beliefs of excellence of NLP that there is a positive intention behind every behaviour and the key to overcoming the unwanted behaviour (anxiety in this case) therefore is to meet its positive intention some other way and to understand and embrace it.

So what is the positive intention of your child's anxiety?

With many children, I just explain that we want both parts to have a conversation and they just get on with it. Sometimes all it takes is for the scared/worried part to be heard and for the other part to reassure it that it has been heard. When we, as parents, say, 'Don't worry,' that is *us* saying it and although our child loves us they don't feel truly heard.

When both parts have been heard and the anxiety has been reassured, invite your child to put both hands on their heart and breathe in a colour that for them represents peace between the two parts, or agreement.

Once your child has mastered this exercise, it's quite an easy one for them to do for themselves.

Mindful breathing

I love this 5-finger breathing exercise for anxiety.

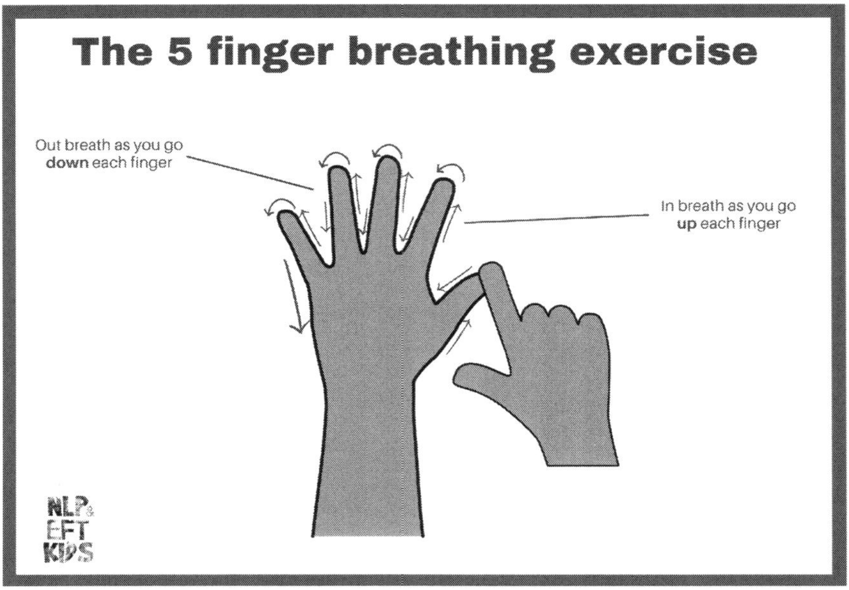

Hold up your left hand, fingers splayed.

- Take the index finger of your right hand and start at the base of your little finger.
- Breathe in as you go up the little finger
- Breathe out as you go down the other side
- Breathe in going up the ring finger
- Breathe out going down the other side
- Breathe in going up the middle finger
- Breathe out going down the other side
- Breathe in going up the index finger
- Breathe out going down the other side
- Breathe in going up the thumb
- Breathe out going down the other side

Now go back the other way returning to the base of the little finger.

Children can do this quietly under their desk or table at school.

Mindfulness Jar

Take a clean empty jar and fill it with water.

Now get a selection of different colour glitter.

Ask your child to imagine that the jar represents their mind. This is a mindfulness jar.

They are to think about the different feelings they have in their mind and give each one a colour then put an amount of each glitter for that emotion in their jar.

Put the top on firmly.

Now shake the jar and watch all the different colours mix together in a whirling mess of colour. Then watch as they gradually settle on the bottom of the jar.

Explain that our mind can be like this with our thoughts and feelings in a chaotic mess but when we stop and breathe we can just quietly watch as they all settle and the water goes completely clear again.

Journaling/Gratitude Diary

Lots of children and adults too really benefit from keeping a journal. I don't mean a diary of what we've done that day.

When children go to bed thinking about things that have happened that day that they didn't like, they dwell on them during the night and wake up feeling anxious about going to school the next day.

Instead, encourage them to think about three things they're grateful for, things that have gone well.

They might like to journal, draw or write a poem about what has gone well that day or things they'd like to think about.

Thought Diary

CBT (cognitive behaviour therapy) is all about the connection between our thoughts and our emotions how

Core beliefs ➤ assumptions ➤ automatic thoughts ➤ emotions

By paying attention to the thoughts that they have in situations where they experience anxiety, they can actively decide to change that thought to a more empowering one by challenging it. So encourage your child to keep a thought diary and record the anxious thought then ask themselves

- What evidence do I have for this thought?
- Is it always true, no exceptions, ever?
- Am I jumping to a conclusion?
- Or catastrophising?
- Is this really all about me?
- Would someone else think the same, though?

- What would a friend say in this situation?
- Is there another explanation?

Then intentionally decide to change the thought to a better one.

The fake laugh

Crazy as this might seem, the fastest way to change your state is to change your breathing. If the situation permits and it isn't completely inappropriate, suggest to your child that a good hearty belly laugh will clear the stress of anxiety. When we feel anxious we tend to hold our breath and, in doing this, we hold in the feeling and make it worse. Instead try laughing (singing works as well but is probably even less possible in most stressful or anxious situations). I've worked with teenagers who have successfully been able to clear exam nerves by laughing and joking with their friends before going into an exam and others who have done this when they were about to take part in a sports event they felt anxious about.

EFT Tapping script for Anxiety

Use this script when you see that your child or teen, looks, sounds or does something you would normally associate with being anxious.

I would suggest they stop whatever they are doing and sit down. Take a pause. And **breathe.**

Ask them to put their hand on their heart and breathe in for the count of six and out for the count of six. They might find it helpful to do this with their eyes closed or looking down. This way they can more easily block out other people and focus on what they are feeling and on their breathing.

The fastest way of changing state (mood or state of mind) is to change your breathing. Simply by stepping away from the thing that's creating the anxiety and focusing on the breathing will help your child feel calmer and more in control. It enables them to be fully present in the moment rather than dwelling on the future – what might happen (it is unknown) or the past (which has happened already so it can only be a perception of what happened). The present is the only time that is known. This mindful moment has a way of stabilising a child.

Breathing is something your child can control. They cannot control whatever is making them anxious but they can control their response to it.

EFT is an energy healing therapy and tapping moves the body's energy, clearing blocked energy pathways that have been disturbed by negative thoughts. It is therefore a good idea to have water to drink before, during and after tapping. The body is mostly energy and water so it makes sense to increase the water supply at this time.

Now let's move on to clear the anxious feeling. Script 1 is a very simple script that can be used for anything.

Script 1

You can see your child is anxious/worried/scared about something and in the moment you need to calm them down.

Show them how to put their hand out in the karate chop and take the other hand to tap it on the soft part between the little finger and the wrist.

Say:

> "Even though I have these feelings, I love and accept myself anyway."
>
> "Even though the feelings seem big right now, I love and accept myself anyway."
>
> "Even though I don't like these feelings, I love and accept myself anyway."

Tapping through the fingers – on the side of each finger of the left hand with the index and middle finger of the right hand, seven times on each (roughly).

As you tap each finger say what you feel or just say

> 'these feelings'

Or

> 'these bad feelings'
>
> 'these anxious feelings'
>
> 'these scary feelings'

It doesn't matter so long as your child uses their own words and you say the same words as them.

Encourage them to breathe as they tap, and encourage them to drink water.

Another good place to tap is on the collarbone using the same two fingers of each hand. You can even pretend to be Tarzan and thump your chest on the collarbone (gently).

This will calm your child down and it's a very simple script.

Script 2

This script is more complex and will be better for clearing the different aspects of anxiety and be more likely to clear it completely as it covers their feelings in more depth. You would do this with them at a different time, perhaps when you have more time rather than actually in the moment of panic or worry.

So, in order to bring up the feelings, you will need to ask them to think about a time when they felt really anxious. This is called 'tuning in'.

Ask them:

> "Where in your body do you feel this feeling?"

I would not name it as anxiety because that word is rather general and covers a whole mix of emotions: worry, sadness, nervousness, agitation, feeling wobbly, sick and so on. Children don't have the breadth of vocabulary to be that accurate about their feelings so it's better, in my opinion, to start with a more general approach – this feeling or these feelings.

Children will say that they feel feelings in their tummy usually. If they say 'my head' this indicates that they are thinking about the thought rather than the feeling so ask them to guess. Guessing is the way we connect with our subconscious mind and that's where we need to be with tapping. So ask them, "If you could change your thought into a feeling and guess where it might live in your body, where would that be?"

Now say to them:

> "I'm wondering what colour it is."

Our subconscious mind communicates in images and colours. Although I've encountered some adult clients who struggle to find the colour, children readily access it.

Go on to find out more about this feeling.
Is it moving or still?
How big is it? Thinking about fruits, is it grape size, orange, melon?
Is it hard or soft?
What else can you tell me about it?

I note these words down because as we tap, we need to use their words.

Ask what the feeling is called, what is the "I feel......" it could be 'sad', 'worried' or it might be 'angry,' it might be 'unimportant'. The more you do this sort of exercise with your child, the more you will build emotional intelligence so they can readily name their emotions and manage them.

In order to keep track of the intensity of the feeling, it is helpful to get a starting point. So ask your child, on a scale of 0 - 10 how bad is your feeling when zero is nothing, no feeling and 10 is as bad as it gets. Note this so you can track as it goes down.

Now we start tapping. The first part of the process is called the 'set-up'.

Taking one hand in a karate chop position, take the fingers of your other hand and tap on the soft area between your wrist and little finger. Ask your child to repeat your words as you tap. You will need to pause between each phrase as they won't remember the whole thing to repeat it. That's why I've put each phrase on a different line. Remember to only use their words. This is called 'clean language'. Using our own words, even when we feel that's what they must mean, will get in the way of connecting them with their feelings. It may seem counterintuitive to be getting a child to be focusing on their angry or sad feelings but what we are doing here is owning them and loving ourselves even with these feelings.

> "Even though I feel this (colour) (the name they used for their feeling)
> and it's in my (part of the body)
> it's (other words they've used to describe it)
> I love and accept myself anyway."

Here's an example of something a child might have said that we are using for their set- up phrase.

"Even though I feel this red worry
And it's in my belly
And it's hard and round like an orange
I love and accept myself anyway."

We say this 3 times, slowly. The tone to use is quite low and almost hypnotic because we want to be gentle and nurturing, connecting with these unwanted feelings with kindness and acceptance as a part of us that we'd like to heal and clear.

Now for the tapping rounds.

Here is the order of the points. You can also refer to the diagram in the introduction to the book.

As you tap on each point in turn, around 7 times on each, you say the reminder phrase which will be one or two of the words from your set-up phrase. Again, you say the word and your child repeats it. So using my example above, you might use

Red
Red worry
Red in my belly
Hard like an orange
Anger in my belly
And so on.

It will seem repetitive to you and that is how it should be. The repetition will have a calming and hypnotic effect on your child because you're just using their words. Those are the words that connect them with their feelings.

Top of the head
Side of the eye above the nose
Other side of the eye

Under the eye
Under the nose
Under the mouth
Collarbone
Under arm (bra strap line)

Go through this sequence twice and ask them to go back to tapping on the side of their hand so you can check with them what's happening. Tap along with them (as you should be doing throughout this process) because by tapping together you get borrowed benefits; it's like multiplying the effect.

If your child is quite young and they want to, they can tap on their teddy bear or other cuddly comfort toy and this is like them tapping on themselves. This is called 'surrogate tapping'. As they tap on their bear and say their words it has the same effect as if they were tapping on themselves.

So, as you tap on the side of the hand, ask them to check whether there have been any changes.

> "Can I just check, what is the feeling you have now?
> And where is it in your body?
> What is the colour now?
> And the size?
> And anything else about it."

Note the new words. The words may not change much after two rounds but I find that, with children, change can be quite quick. You can also check the SUDs level. That was the number they gave you out of 10 at the beginning. It will have reduced but will still have some way to go.

It's not unusual for anxiety, worry etc. to change as you go through the first two rounds of tapping. Children often experience anger or sadness as they connect to their feelings. When we feel that the emotion has changed, we do another set-up.

> "Even though I feel (name of feeling) now
> And it's (colour)
> In my (part of the body)
> And it's the size of a (name of fruit)
> And it's (anything else about it)
> I love and accept myself anyway."

Then do two more rounds of tapping using the new reminder phrases.

If your child is finding it difficult to follow the tapping points, you can switch to using the finger points.

Putting your hand on one side, using the index finger of one hand, tap each finger of the other hand beside the nail bed, about seven times.

Check again to see what score your child gives to their anxiety.

I might ask now:

> "If there was a colour that you can imagine breathing into your body that would blow away any last (colour) from your (part of their body) what would it be?"

Ask them to close their eyes and put their hand on that part of their body holding the remaining negative colour and ask them to imagine breathing in this new positive colour so that it fills their body and especially the area holding that remaining anxiety or other negative feeling they have.

Then ask them to open their eyes. They should now feel much calmer. Suggest they use this tapping every time they feel any anxiety. If they are in company, at school or with friends they can do the finger tapping.

There is another version of EFT that is done in silence and if any of you work in schools or help out, this is great for situations where you have a lot of children and can't have everyone saying different words at different times because it would be chaotic and not conducive to creating a calm classroom. Once the children have been introduced to EFT as a method, been shown the tapping points and the principles explained the teacher can simply start tapping on the karate chop point to cue the children to follow. Instead of speaking at the set-up and while tapping through the points, each child thinks about what they are feeling and taps to clear it.

Schools using Silent Tapping in this way have found improved levels of calmness, compassion and focus. Many children take the technique home to their families and introduce it there. It may soon become as well known in schools as Mindfulness.

3

Coping with change

I'm going to cover a few specific changes such as a new sibling, divorce/separation and death of a pet. But first I'd like to explain how some children find change more difficult than others.

In Part 1, I explained about the NLP metaprogrammes and how children usually have a preference. Some children like what's familiar, the same as, how things normally are and what they expect. We say they like to 'match'. They tend to look to agree with what's happening and what's said, with ideas proposed and they generally go with the flow. Well, at least they do until there is some change to that flow that they had relied on to stay the same.

Children who match, resist change. It makes them nervous and stressed, and it's tempting to say of them, 'They don't like change,' but beware because it's not a good idea for them to believe that this is their identity because they will open themselves up to being rescued by teachers, friends and extended family, making it difficult for them to embrace change in the future for work and life out in the wider world. Better instead to say when talking about them and to them that change is how we experience new things, after all, they have changed from crawling to walking and from baby milk to solids, from nursery to school and so on.

Focus on the changes that they have accomplished with grace and ease and remind them of how well they did this. The reason to focus on changes they've navigated well is because this is evidence that it is not their identity, it is not a stuck state but one that they just need some skills to help them in some cases. Skills are what we'll focus on here because it is so much better for their self-esteem when you share new skills with them than you rescuing them.

Think of the **Drama Triangle** that has been mentioned in other chapters and is super relevant here. Your child struggling with change is in the Victim role saying, "I can't do this," feeling useless and embarrassed in front of his mates perhaps or crying, pulling away and trying to get to safety.

A parent or teacher is cajoling them, reassuring them that all will be well and promising to stay with them. This is the Rescuer who means well, of course, but basically just confirms that indeed they are right, they actually can't do this alone, they need the Rescuer.

In the Persecutor role is the thing that's new, the situation, the person and if you are trying to persuade them in a way that feels threatening to them, then that persecutor role may be you. It's not unusual for one parent to try to 'rescue' and the other to 'persecute'.

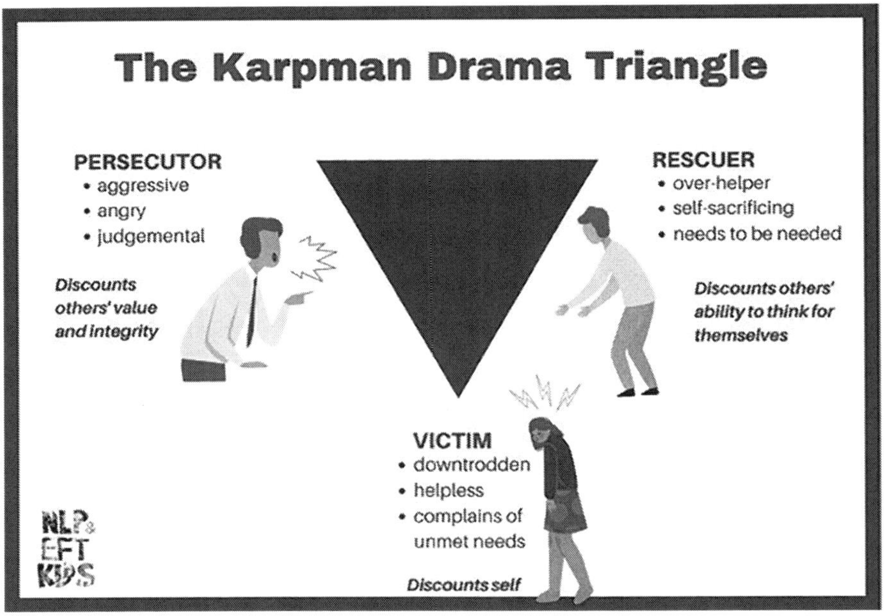

Whatever role you take, though, your child is still in the Victim role and still feels that they can't do whatever it is.

So let's look at how to help them escape the Drama Triangle. Guess what? It's you who has to change. Yes, when the rescuer changes tack, and becomes more of a coach then the victim is free to become a survivor, a problem solver, a child who 'can'. How do you do this?

– Instead of you coming up with the solutions, ask <u>them</u>.

One of the NLP beliefs of excellence is: the map is not the territory. This means that how the world seems to us is different for our child. So they are really the best placed to create a well-formed outcome or solution based on their own map of the world.

It will be important how you deliver the question, "What would you suggest?" or words that suit your child's age and your relationship with them. You need to deliver the question with the belief that they <u>do</u> have the ability to solve this and that you trust them to have the best solution. Of course this will be hard if you've always resolved this issue by rescuing them but think about how they will cope with change when they're on their own. You won't be there when they're at school, on a school trip and certainly not when they are at secondary school or university.

– Focus on when they cope with small changes well so they have evidence that they can cope with change.

Then build on this by reminding them of occasions when they've demonstrated these abilities. You could even use different wording so they can reframe 'change' as something less new and different, and more of a minor alteration to a plan. Some children respond anxiously just to a word like 'change' whereas introducing change as this 'great idea you've had that they will really enjoy' may be greeted differently. How creative and upbeat can you be? It's also about you believing they will enjoy it and they will pick this up in your delivery of the idea.

Note the changes they have made and give them specific feedback on these so they can learn from them. This will really help. By specific feedback I mean instead of simply saying 'well done' you need to mark out the abilities or skills they've used such as

- You really listened well to what I told you about what will happen
- You were brave about the change of plan
- You were full of good ideas for how to manage this change
- You had a positive attitude about having a new teacher

Focus on the positive outcome.

So often children focus on the change itself and see it as a block, but when you can talk with them about what that change will mean for them and the positive outcome, they can see beyond the change.

I tend to use the NLP **submodalities** for this. For example, if their block is like a wall, ask them to imagine the wall is transparent and they can see what's on the other side. What is it? What fun will it be? Or imagine the wall being made of ice cream, eat it or let it melt and see what they will enjoy on the other side of the wall. Can they push the wall down, or make a hole in it? When you focus with them on the positive aspect, and when that is greater than the thing that's stopping them, the odds are that they will favour the change.

You now have three new ways to cope with change for a child who is resistant or a match child. So let's look at different changes that you will encounter on this wonderful parenting journey.

Arrival of first sibling

I'm going to focus on this because it can be the worst and most dramatic change for the first born, to find they are going to have a sibling. It isn't always a disaster in their little mind but it may be. So, let's prepare.

You've been pregnant before so there's nothing new for you but your child has no idea of this process. Why is mummy getting fat? Why is she being sick? Why is she always tired and grumpy? Why is everyone talking about her tummy? It's very confusing. If your child is over 4yrs of age and able to understand, then show them pictures and talk about how baby is developing. This will help but nothing prepares them for an actual baby in your arms.

They have been the centre of your universe for some years perhaps, certainly all their life, which is the important thing to them. Why on earth would you need another? Aren't they enough?

Nothing will ever be the same for child number 1. It is a threat to survival and the ultimate change at a time when you have so many demands on you from the new baby. Babies are enormously demanding day and night so you will be physically tired and emotionally drained. The activities you used to enjoy with your child will be curtailed perhaps even stopped if you've had a difficult birth. Perhaps your partner will do them. This can be very difficult because despite your best intentions, as far as they are concerned, they are being fobbed off with the understudy. This can cause problems between you and your partner potentially as their attempts to help are not necessarily welcomed.

Inevitably some jealousy will occur because they just want your attention. They may even try to hurt the baby to get your attention because, at least that way, they get some attention. They don't really want to help you with the baby or be the older brother or sister, they feel they are still the baby and want the special treatment they are used to.

So what's the answer? If you have a gap of more than four years between children it means that the older child is distracted by school, new friends and the fact that they have greater reasoning power. This means they understand the physical demands of the baby and don't feel so emotionally threatened, but of course this four year gap isn't always what a family wants.

Focus on the things that really matter, the special things you do with your child, so that these things continue to remain yours. If you can get the baby to take a bottle of expressed milk or if you're using formula, you can have more flexibility to do this. Flexibility is key. The more creative you can be with juggling the baby so you can focus on your older child the better. They won't mind if the house is a mess, so long as they get time with you.

I sometimes say delegate/ dump/do when it comes to time pressures like this. Delegate those things you don't have to do yourself, and let's face it, there's probably lots of things that can be done by someone else, if only for a few months. Dump those things that weren't important anyway. People will understand and in the long run those things weren't that important perhaps. Do the things that matter.

Make as few changes as possible so your older child feels secure. They will probably regress to being a baby sometimes as they think that's what gets your attention so ignore this and pay attention when they are being their normal self so this isn't encouraged.

If you have a 'choices' child (see Part 1 NLP metaprogrammes) you can involve them in making choices as they'll enjoy this. Maybe they can choose some food for the baby, choose music to play and dance to, story books and clothes. There may be some things they have less choice over now there are two children, so allow choice where you can. If your child is more 'process' they can help make a to do list for the day and tick things off.

Set a **compelling outcome** for each week because each week will be different. Remember that you need to decide what you want for the week ahead. Write it down here

....

Now let's just check that you've worded it as a 'towards' statement saying what they <u>do</u> want rather than an absence of something or less of something.

Check that this is in your control.

It is an alarming fact of life that babies are not in our control. Nor are your children. So remember that the only thing in your control is your response to what happens. Do you need to rewrite your compelling outcome? Do it here.

....

We are going to apply the SMART goal criteria. I expect you are familiar with them.

S is for Specific

Is your outcome a bit vague? If you've used words like *better* or *calmer* these comparatives are not specific. Aim for something more 'small chunk'. If you need to make a change, write it down here.

....

M is for Measurable

How will you measure whether you have achieved your outcome? There needs to be a way so you can feel great about having achieved it. Goodness knows, it's hard enough to achieve anything with a baby and a toddler around. Do you need to scale it down?

....

A is for Achievable

Can you achieve this? Be reasonable, have you set yourself a tough task? Again, take this opportunity to scale it back if you've aimed high.

....

R is for Relevant

There's no point setting an outcome that doesn't make much difference to you so make sure your outcome is something that really is compelling in that you will feel great when you achieve it, however inconsequential it might be for someone else. This is your outcome. If you love reading and you've set a goal of reading one page in a book, if it matters to you then it is a compelling outcome.

Just write Yes! If it is relevant to you ....

And maybe why?

....

How will it make you feel when you have achieved it?

....

Setting small achievable, meaningful outcomes will get you through each week and as each week goes by, you'll be able to celebrate these small steps towards feeling calm.

Another NLP principal that will help is **Modelling**.

This is where we can learn from what others do. Plenty of other parents have been through this stage and pass on their tips and ideas, this is a good starting point.

The crucial piece of information we need though is the belief they had about the thing they did. Everyone has different values, so it won't necessarily work to model someone with different values to you. What do you think their belief is about being a good parent during this stage? Find someone whose values are the same as yours and follow their tips.

When mine were little I used to **journal** as it was my way of talking to someone even if it was just to myself. There are always bad times, sad times and mad times but these rarely last for the whole day, so being able to dump your thoughts into a journal is a great way to offload and sometimes laugh about it later. You can buy Gratitude journals where you can note what you're grateful for every day which is a positive approach but I quite like also being able to rant. You certainly can't go shouting at babies or little children so shouting into your journal can feel very therapeutic.

I didn't know **EFT tapping** when mine were little but I wish I had. Here's a little tapping script for times when things aren't so great. The beauty of tapping is that you can introduce it to your older child as a way to help them when they may be feeling a bit left out, sad or cross.

Usually we 'tune in' but here I'm going to assume you are already in the state you want to change through tapping. So we'll go straight to the set-up stage. Just think about what you're feeling or if it's your child you're tapping for, what they are feeling. Give the feeling a name and then think about where in the body it is and what colour it is. As I'm guessing you have a small child with you, you could ask "if it's an animal, what animal is it?" They love this.

Tapping your dominant hand against your non-dominant hand on the karate-chop point between the base of your little finger and your wrist, tap it while you say,

> "Even though I am feeling .... and it's .... (colour) and it's like a .... (animal), I love and accept myself anyway."

It's important if you're tapping for yourself that you use these words but if you're tapping with a small child you could alter them to "I love myself anyway" or "I'm OK for now," or "I'm a good boy/girl."

Say these words 3 times and then start tapping either on the body or on the fingers. It doesn't matter which but lots of small children prefer the body and older ones prefer the fingers. Show them the points and ask them. The full process of using EFT is in Part 1.

As you tap through the points just repeat the reminder phrase which will be their feelings. We mostly focus on the negative feelings because these are the ones we want to clear.

After some tapping, you'll find they (and you) feel much calmer.

Let me share a couple of emergency tapping points.

Cross/angry feelings can be cleared by tapping with both fists under the arms like a monkey.

Anxious/sad feelings can be cleared by tapping with both fists on the collarbone point, again like a monkey.

They knew a thing or two, these monkeys!

Another way to remind yourself that this is simply a temporary stage is by using a **Time Line**.

Imagine a line along the floor. Your older child can join you in this but indulge yourself on your own the first time. The line goes from your own birth to an age when you'll be well past this stage and they are both at school full time. Now stand on the point representing today, this time, the present.

Think about how you feel right now.

Now take a moment and head into the future on your time line to a point when things are feeling calmer or whatever the feeling is that you'd like to go to. Stand on that point on the Time Line and

- See what you see
- Hear what you hear
- Feel what you feel

As if it's happening right now. Notice what you're doing, who you're with, what's going on and see yourself in that state you want to be in.

Now go to another point further along the time line in the future and again repeat that process of associating into that time as if it's today, noticing everything about it.

Staying there, just turn to face your present day point on the time line and imagine what you'd like to say to that person. Say it. You might like to write it down here.

....

Meditation

A lot of people love a gentle meditation. It can be a special thing to do with your older child together at bedtime or when the baby is napping. There are loads to choose from on YouTube so you can ring the changes (unless you have a 'match' child of course in which case they will prefer the same one each night).

Compassion Break

Last but not least, here's a lovely 'compassion break' just for you.

Put both hands on your heart and express how you feel. You may need to do this silently if your child is close by but it is a lovely little exercise to teach them, too. It is a real gift for children to be able, from an early age, to accept and express their feelings before the feelings build up into something uncontrollable. We all know where that leads, don't we?

> "I feel ...."

When you've completely run out of feelings, stretch both hands out in front of you as if offering those feelings up to the universe.

> "Right now, there are parents/children just like me feeling the exact same thing as me all over the world. I am not alone."

Take a moment to imagine all those other people feeling the same. It's good to know you're not alone. When I do this with children we name all the countries they can think of where there are other children thinking the same as them.

Now think about what you need.

> "Right now what I need is a ...."

Whatever you need, be it a hug, a kiss, a cup of tea, a sleep, a run or to do something special for yourself, try to do it if you can. This is also a useful exercise for children to acknowledge what they feel and what they need from as young an age as possible.

Divorce/separation/death of a parent

This is another huge change for children and, unlike the arrival of a sibling, this change may not be something you wanted, so it may be a trauma to you as well. You cannot reassure them that everything will be OK because you probably don't know that it will, but the most important thing to convey to them is that this has nothing to do with them. They are not responsible for what has happened. Children do blame themselves, even thinking that if they had done what they were told or been quieter, better behaved, smarter, less annoying, then this wouldn't have happened. This is because children believe they are the centre of your world, and to some extent, of course, they are, which is why when something goes badly wrong, then they believe it must have something to do with them.

This is probably the next biggest cause of distress in their life after the birth of a sibling. It makes a difference in their life on a daily basis and, not having one parent there whenever they want them, will be a huge loss. Children would prefer two unhappy parents than one happy parent because, as children, they don't understand. You may find that they revert to toddler behaviour such as bedwetting and eating problems or they may withdraw in hurt and overwhelm.

If you can, focus on a 'compelling outcome' by using a **Time Line** with them. First, you need to discuss this with them in order to ensure it is both 'towards' (something they want) and within their control. I've worked with a number of children who have set their hearts on wanting mummy and daddy to get back together but we were able to reframe this into something they could control which was how they wanted to feel about it.

Ask them to imagine a line representing time laid out on the floor out in front of them and they should stand on a point representing today. Ask them to tell you their compelling outcome, how they'd like to feel.

Now ask them to go to a time in the future when they will feel like this. This may seem impossible for them but ask them to guess when they might feel better than they do right now.

When they are standing on that point ask them what's happening, how old they are, who's there, what they're doing and get them to associate into the feeling: see what they see, hear what they hear and feel what they feel.

I think it's a good idea to **anchor** this feeling.

Ask them to simply put their thumb and index finger together to make an OK sign as they think about this happier time in the future while they are standing on that future time.

Then they could turn towards the point representing the present and reassure their younger self that things will get better. Some children like to write a letter to their younger self, others have an imaginary conversation. Maybe they can share some insight as to what they might be doing in the future.

Then they can go back to today's point on the line and talk about what they can do today to start to make the change.

Some children like to **journal** as if they're sharing their life with the missing parent. Resist the temptation to read it as this will betray their trust.

Tapping will also help in this situation. Here's a tapping script that might be useful. Get them to tell you how they feel if you are unsure of what words to use as you'll need to use their words during the tapping.

Remember to ask them to 'tune in' to whatever they are feeling right now and give the feeling a name, a colour and tell you where they're feeling it in their body. Then using that information, you can do the set-up.

> "Even though I'm feeling .... (their feeling word) and it's .... (colour) in my .... (part of the body) I love and accept myself anyway."

You say this 3 times while you're tapping on the karate-chop point.

Now start the rounds of tapping on the body. Check the diagram in Part 1. Use the reminder phrases that they have told you at the beginning and, starting with the top of the head, tap all the points about 6 or 7 times as you say the words. Make sure you tap with your child, leading the process by saying their words and they repeat them.

After two rounds, check how they're feeling. It is not surprising to find that feelings change, especially in such circumstances. Sadness can often turn to anger. If this happens, repeat the set-up process with the new words and do two more tapping rounds with them.

Check again to find out how they are. Hopefully they feel much calmer. It might be helpful for them to think about a colour that represents love and breathe that in.

I ask, "If there was a colour that, for you, represents love or the feeling you'd like to have, what would it be? Now close your eyes and put your hand on your heart as you breathe that colour into your heart space and fill it up as you breathe in for five and out for five, filling your heart with that beautiful colour of love."

Some changes are so terrible that it can be difficult to ever imagine that there will be some resolution or that you or they will be OK. You can use **modelling** to help here.

Is there someone you know who has been through something similar to what you're experiencing now? Ask them about it and explore how they managed to support their family and heal themselves. Those who have been through painful times will understand how you are feeling and will remember the poignant first steps along the road to recovery. No one else's situation will be exactly the same as yours but by sharing the pain with others who know what you're going through, some models of excellence may be picked up that you can apply to you and your family. What you need, essentially, is the belief of excellence, their belief in the situation that has kept them going through the dark times.

Here are several NLP tips that might also help;

- Use 'towards' rather than 'away from' language with your children. Rather than talk about what you no longer have, focus instead on what you <u>do</u> have and joint goals you have discussed and agreed.
- Grief sometimes distorts images of the past and of the future. Notice when you use words like 'never' and 'always', 'everyone', 'better' and so on. These generalisations and distortions can be taken quite literally by children and aren't usually a fair reflection of the situation.
- Use their preferred language, visual, auditory or kinaesthetic to discuss their feelings.
- Step into their shoes to understand their territory. How they see their new world will be quite different from how you see it.
- As they steadily make progress towards coping with the changes, use anchors with them to remind themselves at less good times that there have been some improvements.

However bad things may seem now, if you have a desirable outcome that you agree with your children and tie it down to specifics you all have something to aim for. When you talk through with them what they think would be something to aim for, write down all suggestions and agree which ones will work. Then post it up somewhere so that everyone can see it and work towards it. Younger children may like to draw a picture of their desirable outcome so post that up as well.

I love **vision boards** and it is a great way to see how feelings and thoughts change as we heal from our hurts. Take a piece of card and gather pictures, words, splashes of colour, or whatever your child wants to use, and arrange them as a collage on the card. Then put it up in their room. Write the date on the back. In years to come, they can look back and notice the healing journey.

We all want our children to have a happy childhood but that frequently is not possible through death, divorce, illness and separation. There are many books available on these themes and it helps for children to read them and know that they are not the only ones suffering. They also provide child models for them so they can learn from those who have been through a similar experience.

Death of a pet

Pets give unconditional love in a way that parents and siblings don't. Whatever we've done, they are there for us. However grumpy we are, they still love us. They listen to our troubles, comfort us in our sadness and loneliness and when no-one else will listen, our pet understands.

Even the most monosyllabic teenager, however 'cool' they are, can be reduced to tears at the death of their pet. This can even be the case where they don't appear to have been very close to them. Children maybe take it for granted that their pet will always be there, though at a conscious level they know they will not.

The emotions we're dealing with here will be sadness, loss, feeling alone and coping with change of course as they miss the family member that has passed.

Tapping will be the most effective way to support them at this time and maybe the whole family can tap together but your pet will mean something different to each of you so be prepared to tap separately.

If you are saying goodbye to your pet, you can actually tap on your them, tap lightly down the spine from the back of the neck (do not tap on their face) using two fingers each side of the spine and finish at the tail. This will be calming and reassuring. It will also have the effect of calming your child through 'borrowing the benefits' (described in Part 1).

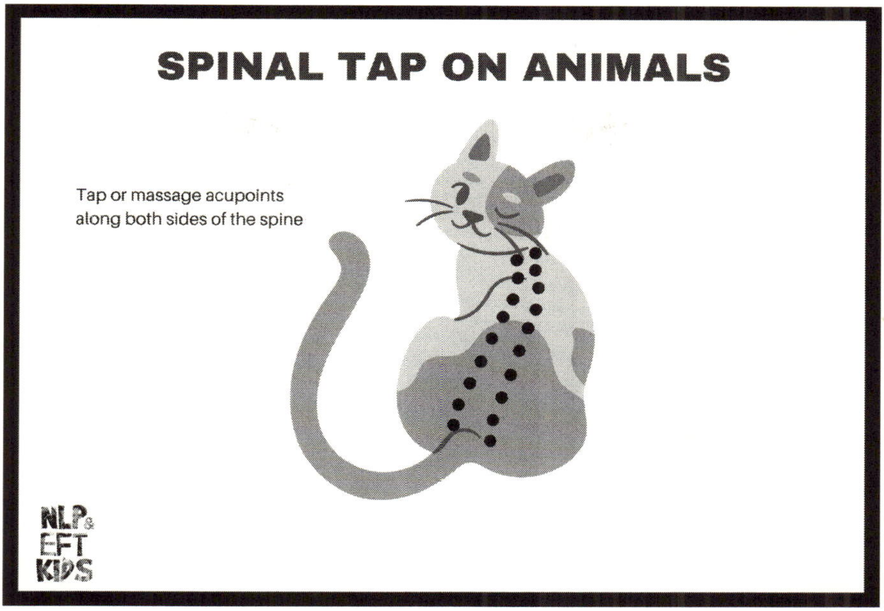

You can tap with your child of course at all stages, from knowing their pet will be 'put down' through to helping them through the grieving process.

Suggest to them,

> "Shall we try a new way I know to help you with what you're feeling?"

Step 1

Ask

> "What would you call the feeling?"

> "If it had a colour, what colour is it?"

> "What size is it, if it were a fruit, what size, is it grape size, apple or melon?"

> "Is it moving or still?"
>
> "Is it hard or soft?"

We want them to give us all the words that describe this feeling of theirs so we can get rid of it.

Finally when you have extracted all you can from them, ask them,

> "If 10 was as bad as it gets and zero was nothing at all, what number would you give this feeling right now?"

Write the number down so we know when it's reduced but it's unlikely to drop to zero if their pet has only recently passed, especially if it was unexpected.

Step 2 – Set-up

Use the diagram in the EFT basics section at the front of the book to remind you of the tapping points.

Ask them to hold out their non-dominant hand (the one they don't write with) as if they were doing a karate chop. Then taking their dominant hand they tap lightly on the fleshy part of the other hand between the base of the little finger and the wrist.

As they do this you can lead them through the set-up using their words.

> "Even though I have this (feeling) in my (part of the body) and it's (colour) I am a good boy/girl."
>
> "Even though I have this (colour) (size) (feeling) in my (body part) I am a good boy/girl"

And then again for a third time, pausing to breathe because things shift quickly for children,

> "Even though I have this (feeling) and it's (colour) and it's in my (body part) I am a good boy/girl"

Step 3 – Tapping rounds

We start at the top of the head using the dominant hand, tapping lightly on the crown and saying the words they used to describe their feelings.

These are the points;

Top of the head
Eyebrow
Side of the eye
Under the eye
Under the nose
Under the mouth
Collarbone
Under the arm

Then we go back round a couple more times.

Step 4 – Check in

Ask your child to go back to tapping on the karate chop point and ask them what their SUDs level is now, this is the number they gave you at the start.

Check whether the colour has changed, the size, is it still static or moving, is the feeling still the same?

It's possible the feeling may have changed.

In that case if it's changed quite significantly then repeat the set-up with the new words. In the case of the death of their pet, expect sadness to turn to anger, then possibly back to sadness.

Step 5 – Finishing

Ask your child what SUDs level they'd like to get to as they may want to hold onto some sadness and this is understandable.

Also ask them how they'd like to feel, what would a good feeling be for now?

What colour is that feeling?

Ask them to take those three deep breaths as they put their hands to their chest or heart and say,

> "Now breathe in this colour through your body taking it into all the parts that need that .... (whatever the feeling was that they'd like to feel).Then remember to do this whenever you need to."

Vision Board

Why not help your child by making a small collection of photos of them with their pet and make a collage for their room or an album for them to keep for themselves to help them remember the relationship they had with their pet.

Whatever big change your child experiences is a form of grief and loss.

A really nice exercise that I learnt a few years ago is the **Heart to Heart** where you invite your child to go to an imaginary special place, maybe a bench in a park, a beach, a log in a wood, somewhere quiet and peaceful and wait for their loved one to join them, a person or a pet they are grieving for, it can even be someone still alive but whom they don't see as much as they'd like. When they are there they can reach out their hand and imagine placing it on their loved ones heart and then say all they want to say to them. Feel the love being accepted and taken in by them.

Then allow the loved one to place their hand (or paw) on your child's heart and imagine what they want to say to your child. Be still and quiet as they do that. If they say they don't know, ask them just to wait and it will come to them. They may find it difficult the first time, but with practise they will build this connection. They should accept the love offered and take it into their own heart.

Then imagine placing them and their loved one in a bubble of love. Ask them what colour they would like the bubble to be. Imagine that bubble and that special place with the special person that they love and they can go to it in their imagination whenever they want.

EFT general tapping script for change

There will be times when there are changes that children are struggling with that may be more minor than those I've just outlined and given you specific scripts for.

So let's start with a set-up although if they are experiencing distress right now, just head on to the set-up or start the tapping rounds. Remember you only really need the tune in if you're teaching them tapping or if the thing that's upset them happened in the past, even a few hours ago. If it has just happened you don't need to tune in because they already are!

Tune in

Ask them to recall the thing, whatever the change was, that upset them by putting their hands to their heart and breathing into it, with eyes closed.

- Then ask them to tell you
- What's the feeling
- What colour is it
- Where in the body is it
- Size – grape, orange, melon or mouse/ dog/ elephant or use arms to indicate

Set-up

> "Even though I have this (colour) (feeling) in my (part of the body) when something changes, I love and accept myself anyway"

Do this three times.

Tapping rounds

Use their words as you tap around the body on the tapping points. About 6 or 7 per tapping point.

Just to remind you, they are;

Top of the head
Eyebrow point
Side of the eye
Under the eye
Under the nose
Under the mouth
Collarbone
Under arm

Do two rounds and then check back on the karate chop point. What's going on? What are the thoughts and feelings now?

I think I'd be inclined to pause and ask your child if they had to guess at an earlier age when they felt like this, when would it be? I'd be wondering what might have happened to create this anxiety around change.

If they do have a memory, repeat the tune in with this memory and then do the set-up and tapping rounds with it to see if you can clear an early imprint of their belief about change.

If they don't then do a 9 step gamut

Find the groove on the hand between the little finger and the ring finger of your non-dominant hand. Use the index and middle finger of your dominant hand to tap gently on that groove. As you do this, you need to also:

- Open eyes
- Close eyes
- Drop eye gaze down to your left
- Drop eye gaze down to your right
- Circle eyes clockwise
- Circle eyes anticlockwise
- Hum a tune
- Count to 9
- Hum a tune

Then go back to the karate chop point to check SUDs level and clear any remaining negative emotions with another set up and two rounds of tapping. This time use the fingers as this will be easy for them to replicate at school.

As a general help to children who struggle with change, note and mark out when they respond well to a change, however small it is so that you gently challenge their assumption that they find change difficult.

4

Fear of Failure

Many children fear failure and you can see this in their reluctance to put their hand up in class, and in their avoidance of new things such as initiating conversations with other children they don't know.

The first thing to think about is how you manage failure yourself because this is how children learn from you. If you are someone who would never admit to any failures in front of your children then it's hard to know how they will know what to do themselves.

One of the NLP presuppositions is that there is no failure, only feedback. In other words what we're doing is reframing a mistake as a learning. We are learning how to get it right, how to do it better next time.

This means being curious and when things go wrong, instead of feeling bad and downhearted to think about what the learning is. The **feedback sandwich** is a great place to start.

Step 1 – Overall, what went well?

It can be hard, in the moment of feeling abject failure, to look at what happened in a positive way but this is where you can help your child. Resist the temptation to tell them what the positives were, use questions like this,

> "I'm wondering in all this, what positives there might be?"
>
> "If there was a positive, what would it be?"
>
> "Who's the most positive friend you have? What do you think they'd notice?"

> "I hear you. It sounds terrible, but can you think of even one good thing that came out of it?"

We want them to know that we understand and we hear them but that when we dig a bit deeper, we can find some learning.

Step 2 – This is where we find the rich learnings.

What will they do differently next time?
What will they do more of?
What will they do less of?

It's important that they explore options. Here's a great way of doing that.

Exercise

Put a wastepaper basket in the middle of the room.

Get out some felt pens and scraps of paper, no need to use the best paper.

Ask your child to think of all the learnings they've gained from what happened. What could they do differently next time? They will want to write things down on the paper and throw each one in the waste paper basket. It doesn't have to be a waste paper basket by the way, just something into which they can throw the scrunched-up pieces of paper.

When they can't think of any more ideas, stop, and give them a good old mix up.

Now ask your child to take them out one by one and read them out. They should then give each idea a score out of 10 for how good it is.

You will end up with lots of pieces of paper with ideas and scores. Lay them out in order of how great an idea each one is and decide which they will try first, the next time something similar happens.

It will be tempting to give an opinion of whether you think that idea is also great, but it is their idea and they know their own environment, friends and so on. So long as ecologically their idea is sound and will not adversely affect anyone and is not illegal then they could give it a go.

Step 3 – Final finish on a high

Now they can put the top slice on that sandwich and finish with the feeling that they have managed to get a good learning experience. Perhaps they have stepped out of their comfort zone, or taken a risk. This is good to learn from.

I think **EFT tapping** is a great tool for children to use if they fear failure.

EFT Tapping script for fear of failure

I'm going to assume they are at home with you at the time you are aware that they are fearing failure, that's certainly the ideal opportunity to introduce them to the technique rather than at school.

You notice they seem worried about something new they are about to do, or a test or exam, a new experience perhaps or a change they weren't expecting. You might say,

> "Shall we try a new way I know to help you with what you're feeling?"

Step 1

Ask them to put their hands on their heart or to their chest, wherever they feel most comfortable, and close their eyes. A good way to start this process is to breathe in for four and out for four, three times, to really encourage the energy in the body to wake up and get ready to move.

Ask them to think about the thing they're worried about and anticipate the worst that could happen. Yes, we want to create a worst-case scenario so we can tap and clear it away.

Now we need to know about this feeling. It's helpful to write down the words they use because you will need them for the next stage

> "Where in your body are you feeling this feeling?"
>
> "What would you call the feeling?"
>
> "What colour is it?"
>
> "What size is it, if it were a fruit, what size, is it grape size, apple or melon?"
>
> "Is it moving or still?"
>
> "Is it hard or soft?"

We want them to identify all the words that describe this feeling of theirs so they can get rid of it.

Finally, when you have extracted all you can from them, ask:

> "If 10 was as bad as it gets and zero was nothing at all, what number would you give this feeling right now?"

Write that number down so we can check that it drops down to as close to zero as we can get it.

Step 2 – Set-up

Use the diagram in the EFT basics section at the front of the book to remind you of the tapping points but I'll try and remind you as we go along.

Ask them to hold out their non-dominant hand (the one they don't write with) as if they were doing a karate chop. Then taking their dominant hand they tap lightly on the fleshy part of the other hand between the base of the little finger and the wrist.

As they do this you can lead them through the set-up using their words.

> "Even though I have this (colour) (feeling) in my (part of the body) I am a good boy/girl."

> "Even though I have this (colour) (size) (feeling) in my (body part) I am a good boy/girl."

And then again for a third time, pausing to breathe because things shift quickly for children.

> "Even though I have this (feeling) and it's (colour) and it's in my (body part) I am a good boy/girl."

Step 3 – Tapping rounds

We start at the top of the head using the dominant hand, tapping lightly on the crown and saying the reminder phrase. Reminder phrases are words from the first step we did when they described the feeling so they will just be words like the colour, the size, anything about the nature of it, whether it is hard or soft, moving or static, and where it is in the body. For example you might be tapping and saying:

Blue
Hard
In my tummy

Large like a melon
Fear
As you tap round the points.

I'll remind you what they are:

Top of the head
Eyebrow
Side of the eye
Under the eye
Under the nose
Under the mouth
Collarbone
Under the arm

Then we go back round a couple more times.

Step 4 – Check in

Ask your child to go back to tapping on the karate-chop point and ask them what their SUDs level is now, this is the number they gave you at the start.

Check whether the colour has changed, the size, is it still static or moving, is the feeling still the same?

It's possible the feeling may have changed.

In that case, if it's changed quite significantly, then repeat the set-up with the new words.

Step 5 – Finishing

You should be able to get your child down to about a 2 or 3 SUDs level and a much lighter colour.

How I like to finish things is by asking them to take those three deep breaths as they put their hands to their chest or heart and ask them to think of a colour they'd like to 'lighten and brighten' their (colour they last mentioned) in their (part of the body).

> "Now breathe in this colour through your body taking it into all the parts that need reassurance or comfort, (use the words your child will resonate with, words they have used themselves) and do this whenever you need to."

If your child needs to be able to tap at school, use the finger tapping points squeezing the tops of their fingers gently around the finger nail with the dominant hand.

I find **Perceptual Positioning** very useful for fear of failure as it helps children understand the positive intention of their fear.

Preparation

Set up three chairs or cushions and explain that one will be Position 1 (their own perspective on the situation and what they'd like to be able to do), Position 2 is their fear of failure, their limiting belief, the thing that's getting in their way of achieving what they want. Position 3 is an uninvolved bystander or like a CCTV camera.

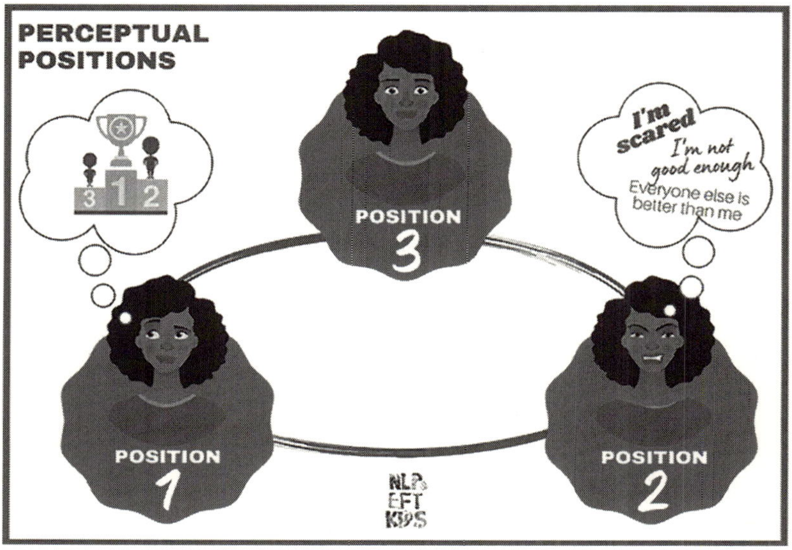

Step 1

Ask them to sit in Position 1 and tell Position 2 what they want to do or how they want to be.

Break state – they stand up and do a little dance or a jiggle, the idea being to mark the change from Position 1 to Position 2 so when they sit in Position 2, they are able to access a different perception (hence perceptual positions).

Step 2

In Position 2, they take on the limiting belief or fear of failure as it is in this chapter. They imagine that this is like another person saying that they will fail, the part of them that fears failure.

Although this might seem like a very odd concept, children do get it and very easily become that part of themselves. The reason it is easy for them is because it's a familiar part of them that they do battle with daily. So in some ways it is a relief to be able to be that part and understand it better rather than trying to fight it.

So Position 2 explains to Position 1 why they will fail, what will happen when they do and how in some way they are there to protect them. They do this by Position 1 and Position 2 talking to each other (putting in a break state each time in between) until there is some clarity for Position 1.

What we're looking for here is for Position 1 to acknowledge the good intent of the fear of failure of Position 2 and be able to reassure them that they can cope with whatever failure means and that they are no longer needed.

What has happened in many cases is that your child may have experienced fear of failure and allowed it to become their identity. Being able to face this part of themselves and remember that they are older now and have more skills, more ability to overcome challenges and more reasons to pursue the goals they want in life, really helps them get rid of their limiting belief.

Step 3

Finally ask them to sit in Position 3, which is like the wise chair, being able to sum up what was said and decide how to move forward in the best way possible.

After doing this exercise I often suggest they do an **eye accessing** exercise whereby they look up to the right and imagine seeing themselves doing the thing they want to do, then at ear level, access what they imagine they will say or what they will hear when they do it. Then they look down to the right and imagine what they will feel when they do it.

This is future pacing, putting their intentions into the future as if they are actually happening and it is like a mental rehearsal for the neural pathways, preparing it for what they want to do.

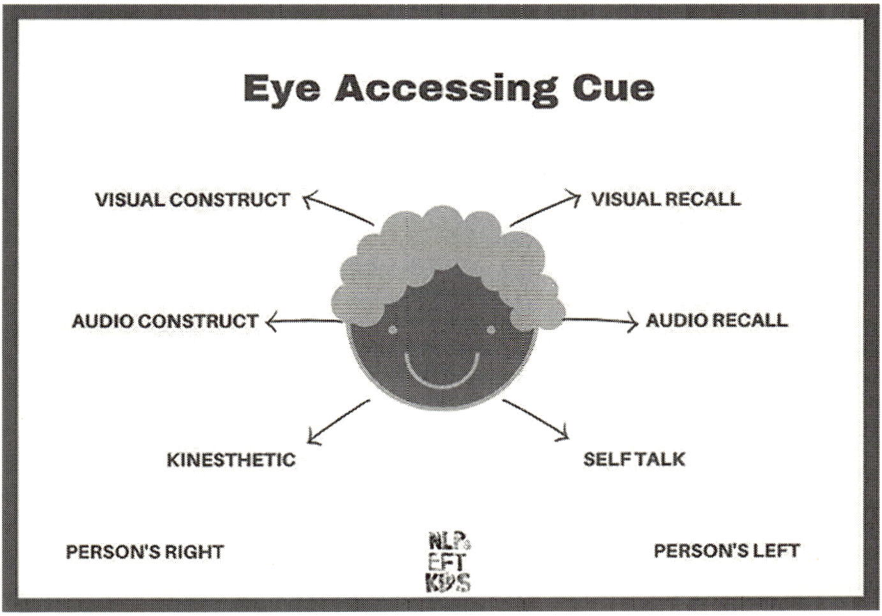

If you've chosen not to do the perceptual positioning exercise, you can still use eye accessing as a stand-alone.

Step 1

Ask your child to think about how they feel about the thing that they fear. To do this they need to look straight in front of them looking up to the ceiling and imagine what they see now that they fear.

Then look straight ahead at ear level and imagine what they hear as they think about doing this thing, who is saying what? What are they saying?

Now look down and connect with the feeling as they think about doing this scary thing.

Straight ahead is where we locate our present state.

Step 2

Now we need to construct a positive outcome instead. Ask them,

> "What would a good outcome look, sound and feel like for you?"

If they aren't sure, or need some help, this is an option,

> "Imagine you are doing this thing you fear but instead you are doing it as you'd like to do it with no fear but instead with confidence that you'll do it well and to your best ability."

Ask them to look to their right-hand side and look up to imagine what they'd like to see, who will be there, what will be happening, they can paint the picture in their mind and add colour, texture and then turn up the light and make it bright and amazing.

Now down a bit to ear level, imagine what they'd like to hear or say. Turn up the volume, make the sounds confident and assured, how they'd like to sound and what they'd like to hear.

Now down to the right, imagine how they would like to feel. Really connect to that desired feeling, the feelings they'd like to feel when they've done this thing confidently and well. Turn up the feeling and feel it as if it's happening right now.

You'll find your child has made a big shift because what we're doing is preparing the neural pathways for the positive outcome. After all, if your child can't even imagine doing this thing as they'd like to do it, then how can it happen?

Let's finish with another lovely technique called the **Self-Compassion break**. Let me talk you through it.

Step 1

Ask your child to put his hands to their heart and acknowledge these feelings of fear of failure. They should say to themselves, "I feel ...." And let it flow into their heart and into their hands.

Step 2

Ask them to put out their hands in front of themselves, as if offering these feelings to the universe, or to the world.

They should say "Right now, all over the world there are boys/girls just like me feeling this fear of failure. I am not alone. Children all over the world are worried about failing, looking stupid, not being smart, being laughed at, getting it wrong, or whatever words they want to use." This is about accepting that they are part of a universe of children who also feel the same, they are not alone.

Step 3

Ask them to put their hands back to their heart and acknowledge what they need right now. "What I need now is ...."

It could be a hug, a snack, who knows, they don't need to say any of this out loud. It's about them accepting the feelings, knowing they aren't alone and knowing how they can self-soothe. This is an important step in you not rescuing them but them being able to rescue themselves.

By introducing children to these techniques, they gain the confidence of knowing they have skills and do not have to be dependent on you for everything. It's a great way to build confidence and encourage them out of their comfort zone knowing they have some skills to cope.

5
Fears and phobias

Children often pick up our phobias and fears quite directly because they have observed our discomfort around particular situations, animals/birds/insects and so on. Despite our attempts to hide them, sometimes we can't, because of the intensity of the reaction and sometimes because, whilst we think we've stayed calm, our children can read us as if we were transparent.

It is possible that a fear or phobia has been masked as an allergic reaction or perhaps even is an allergic reaction but there will still be an awareness for your child that even if it is not their own allergy, there is something potentially dangerous about the thing in question.

Fears are there to keep us safe. Without fear, we would do crazy dangerous things and potentially harm ourselves. I love the way that Elizabeth Gilbert describes fear as being something we should welcome into our car on life's journey and give them a seat in the back. Fear is there to ensure we don't do anything rash like drive too close to the edge of the road or drive in the middle, it makes us drive safely for our own and other passenger's benefit. However, woe betide them should they lean over and try to take the steering wheel or fiddle with the controls.

Children completely understand this and like the idea of fear being there to keep us safe. It leads nicely into a discussion of how their own fear keeps them safe. What is the positive intention of their fear?

Ask your child:

"What would you have to do if you had no fear of this animal?"

"What wouldn't you have to do if you had no fear of this animal?"

An exercise that lends itself well to this issue is **Perceptual Positioning**. Set up three chairs and explain to your child that Position 1 is them, Position 2 is their fear and Position 3 is like a CCTV camera simply observing without emotion.

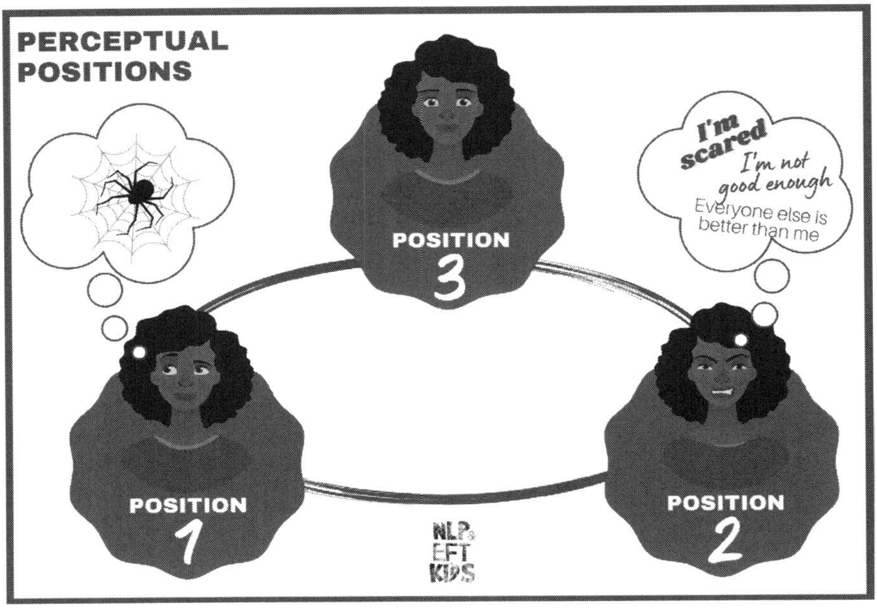

Step 1

Ask your child to sit in Position 1 and tell Position 2 why they don't want their fear, what they want to be able to do and why they are held back by these feelings. Do a break state by having a little dance or a wiggle to mark the change of position.

Step 2

In this chair they imagine they are the fear. They are not the animal or thing they fear but the feeling of fear that is inside them. What would it say to them? What positive intention do they have? Is there any benefit in them being there inside their head?

Step 3

Remember to break state before returning to Position 1 to respond to what their fear said.

The conversation between them and their fear continues until they seem calmer and can appreciate the positive intention of the fear. You should reassure them that it isn't needed, that they are OK. Often children grow up with a fear that becomes like a familiar friend and stays with them for longer than is actually needed. For example, when they were little, dogs might have been a bit scary because perhaps a dog jumped up and knocked them over as a toddler but now they are much taller and unlikely to be knocked over by a bouncy puppy.

Step 4

Break state and move to Position 3 and comment on what you have heard and decide what belief or decision they want to make now they have understood their fear and it's positive intention. Perhaps they can manage without it now?

I think it's helpful and fun to do a Postcard to a Limiting Belief exercise with them to consolidate the learning. Draw a postcard or you can print off a template, perhaps you even have a postcard? Ask them to imagine that their fear has gone away on holiday. It is no longer with them. They should write to their fear suggesting they can stay away because they are much happier without them around. Tell 'fear' what they are now able to do without them to stop them.

I also like to use the **Time Line** for fear of animals because children often say that they have *always* had their fear and, in this way, it is different from fear of failure. They also find it hard to imagine no longer having the fear, so working with a Time Line helps them to appreciate the possibility of change. I explain that the only fear we are born with is a fear of loud noises and a fear of being dropped. Babies are not born with a fear of spiders or monsters under the bed.

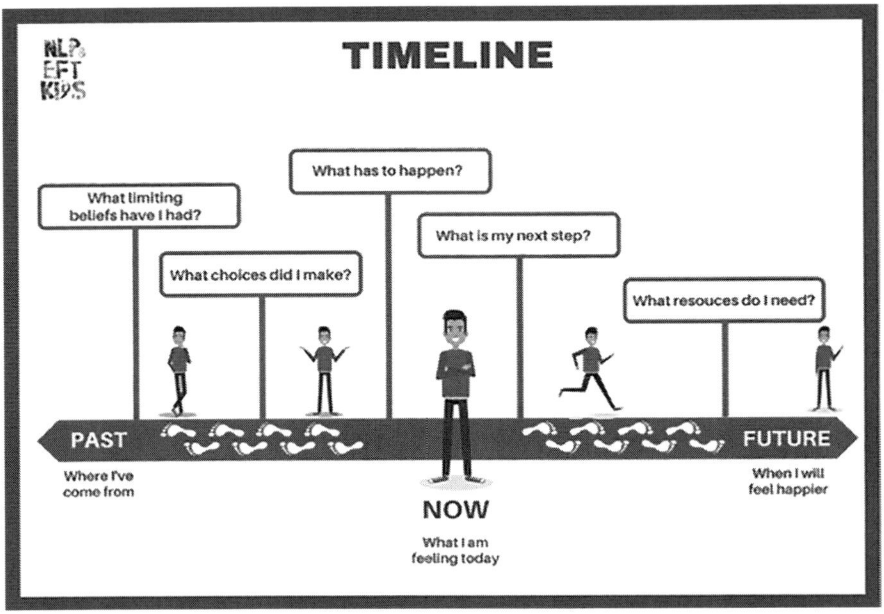

Ask your child to imagine a line along the floor that represents time and it goes from their birth at one end to when they're really old, about 18!

Step 1

Ask them to stand at a point that is roughly the age they are now. How would they like to feel about this animal or thing? What would the resolution look, sound and feel like? We can introduce what we call eye accessing here.

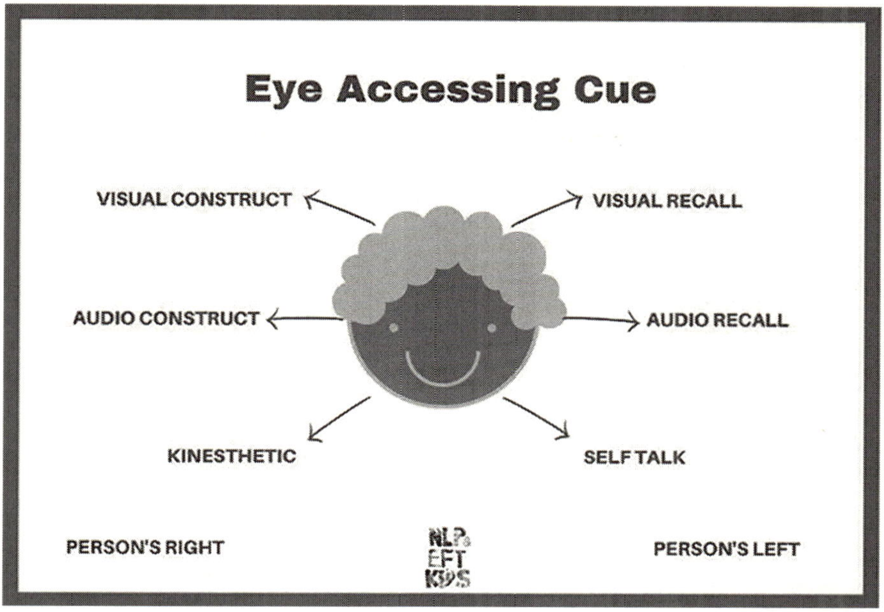

Ask them to look up to the right and imagine that they are looking at the thing they fear as if the fear was now gone. How would they like to look at it?

Then look at ear level to the right imagining what they might say or what they would hear that would be a good result.

Then look down to the right and imagine how they will feel when they get a good result with their phobia.

Having done this, ask them to go to a place on their Time Line where they will feel like this, when they have the result they want.

So ask them now, as they stand in that place, as if they are there in the future right now, how are they feeling, what's happening and check everything is good. What is their belief now about this thing?

Ask them if there was a colour that represented that feeling of (name the word they are using for this positive result) what would it be? Suggest they breathe that colour right through their body and into their heart and feel that feeling throughout their body. When they've done that, ask them to stay where they are but look at the place where they stood as their current age self. What would they like to say to them? Say it.

Another simple exercise you can do and which works well with younger children, is to write a list of **beliefs and facts**. I like to make them funny ones so they enjoy the exercise.

Your list will have some phrases like this:

Homework is boring.
Maths is hard.
My teacher doesn't like me.
Girls talk too much.
Boys are better at football.
Vegetables are disgusting.

And so on.

It's best to use some of the expressions you've heard them say.

Add in a few that relate to their phobia or fear. So for example,

Being in the dark is scary.
All dogs bite.
Spiders are dangerous.
There are monsters under my bed.

Also include some facts:

Then ask them to divide the statements up into facts and beliefs which will usually spark a useful discussion about what constitutes a fact. I usually aim to arrive at some sort of definition around something having to be true for everyone in order for it to be a fact.

Then watch them maybe moving the belief around their phobia from fact to belief. The physicality of doing this is important.

Now ask them to divide up their pile of beliefs into 'limiting beliefs' that stand in our way and don't help us, and 'resourceful beliefs' that help us. Where have they put their phobic belief?

Have a discussion about some of their beliefs.

- Have any changed?
- What caused them to change?
- How could they change their phobic belief?
- What would they like to change it to?
- When will they do this?
- How does it feel to change the belief?
- Are there any others they'd like to change?
- What will be different with these new beliefs?

I particularly like to use EFT Tapping to help children with fears and phobias. Here's a tapping script you can use but please adjust it to suit their age, their fear and the words they use because this makes all the difference.

EFT Tapping script for fears and phobias

Step 1

Tune into the fear if they are not currently frightened. If they are, jump straight to step 2.

They can 'tune in' by putting their hands to their heart and thinking of the thing that they're frightened of.

Ask them where in the body they feel it and the colour. Check how intense it is (SUDs level) by asking 'on a scale of 0-10, how intense is the fear?"

Step 2

Breathe deeply in for the count of 5 and out for the count of 5. Do this 3 times as it helps the body to calm down.

Then start tapping on the karate-chop point as you say, and they repeat after you,

> "Even though I have this (colour) fear of (the thing they fear) and it's in my (part of the body) I am safe right here and right now and I will soon be OK"

Say this phrase 3 times.

Step 3

Now start tapping through the fingers. Although we often use the body points, children need to use the fingers sometimes if they are in a situation where they might feel awkward being seen to be tapping on their head and so on. As they are tapping they need to say the words that they used for the set-up or, if you didn't do a set-up, use words you know they've used about the thing they fear.

- I'm scared of...
- I hate...
- I'm frightened of...
- They are...

Keep tapping and notice how they are feeling. Are they feeling calmer? Ask them? Maybe the feeling has changed a bit. Just change the words as they give you new ones until they are calm and their SUDs level is down to as close to zero as you can get.

Fears and phobias are extreme reactions that come about due to deletions, distortions and generalisations.

Your child has to some extent catastrophised and created their own rule that, for example, they will die, be stung, be trapped, or something else that is in their imagination. It could well have been prompted by them watching something that was too old for their age that you may not even know about because they daren't tell you. The best thing is not to reason with them, because this talks to their conscious mind and the fear is deeper than this and has to be shifted by them. I find using 'clean questions' helps.

- How do you know this?
- Is this always the case?
- Is there ever a time when they are safe?
- Has anyone ever been safe?
- Are all (spiders/dogs/ birds) dangerous?
- Would everyone agree that...?
- What would you say to your friend if they had this fear?
- Is there another way of looking at this?
- Can you make it smaller, lighter, further away in your mind?
- Can you change it to another colour, give it a funny voice or a silly name?

Using the word 'just' can help too. It is a word that minimises which is what we need when a child catastrophises. "It's just a spider," "It's a little spider," or "It's just a dog".

If your child has a **panic attack** the best course of action is to ask them to:

- Look around, what is going on around you?
- Name 5 things you can see.
- Name 5 things you can hear.
- Name 5 things you can smell.
- Who can you see?
- Now imagine your favourite place and see what you see, hear what you hear and feel what you feel.
- Put one hand on your stomach and the other hand on your chest and breathe in through your nose for the count of four and out for four, drawing the breath from your stomach and being aware of it as it moves through your body. Continue until after you feel calm.

For children who feel fears at night please check out the Sleep chapter.

6

Friendship/family relationships

How do we first make friends? What is a friend? Can you remember when you first made friends? Here I'm covering relationships. Mainly friends but of course it's also relevant to sibling relationships, step and other family relationships too. The same principles apply, it's about connecting and building relationships. It's what we want above all.

The word 'friend' can mean something different to each person and changes as we mature. Children frequently say they wish they had more friends and look with envy at someone in the playground who appears to attract more friends than they do. Yet when you ask them how many friends they already have they will reel off at least a dozen names. When you then ask how many more they want, they don't know and say maybe one or two. You then ask for names, and they realise those they thought of already were friends. Here's how a discussion might go and I encourage you to use this style of conversation. It's all about compelling outcomes, focusing on what we want. Children will talk about what they don't want, basically 'no friends' or 'just one friend' because if that friend is off ill they have no one so they need a few to cover for this occasion.

Let's assume that the discussion starts by them saying they wish they had more friends or something along those lines.

If you read Part 1, I explained that one of the metaprogrammes we run is called big chunk/small chunk. Big chunk is when we focus on the concept, the big picture and 'more friends' falls into this category because 'more' is vague rather than specific and 'friends' is a concept too because it's unclear how are they defining what a friend is.

When something is 'big chunk' like this, we cannot get hold of it. It's unachievable because how will we ever know when we have enough? More than how many?

Let's use the **SMART** approach.

First we can ask them to be **SPECIFIC**.

- What is a friend?
- How do you know when someone is a friend?
- Is there just one category of friend?
- How many friends do you have now?
- List them.
- How many more do you want?
- Name them.

I've found this conversation very fruitful because the concept of friendship changes as children get older and, instead of it being a numbers game, it becomes more a matter of quality of friendship. As they get older, their expectations and requirements of a friend change and aspects such as loyalty, honesty and compassion become important. When they were younger, anyone who would play with them was a friend, anyone who invited them to their party or for a play date. So knowing what they want from a friend is a conversation we need to have with our children. That's why I started this chapter asking you the very same question.

You might even find that having had this discussion with you, they are no longer worried about the number of friends they have and value the few they have even more.

How will they **MEASURE** success in this?

Help them to consider whether they want to work on making closer friendships with those they already have or to build a wider network of friends.

This can become a conscious decision for children as they prepare to leave the school for the next stage in their education. In many cases they will be going to a different school from some of their friends so they need to decide whether to build closer friendships with those who will be going to the same secondary school or making the most of the time with friends who will be going to a different one.

Sometimes children measure success against their peers. Who seems to have more friends? This is what we call 'external referencing' when we defer to external cues to make our decisions about ourselves. We look at 'others' not within ourselves.

Encourage your child to think about how their friendships have developed, who seems to have become a closer friend, who may be less so. Also to think about who they are a good friend to themselves, how could they give more, be more?

What is success? Is it a numbers game?

Is it more about having someone who is there for you when you feel a bit down?

Is it someone to go shopping with at the weekend?

What are the signs of a friend? What evidence do you look for to measure whether that is a friend or just another child in your class that you sometimes play with? Maybe that's what a friend is.

Friends are extremely important to children and teens. It's how they know who they are, by constant comparison with others. As they get older, they are more particular, more demanding. Not everyone will be, of course. It may just be enough to have friends to play a game with in the playground.

How **ACHIEVABLE** is it?

What will it take to make more friends?

Can they do it?

How will they do it?

This prompts a really interesting conversation about how we make friends.

It will be different for children of different ages, some children find it quite easy and others find it agonisingly hard.

I've spoken to children who worry about it so much that by the time they get to school they are rigid with fear. They go and sit on the bench in the playground and hunch up, hoping no one will approach yet dreading that they won't. Whilst they desperately want to be part of a group, their fear prevents them from approaching anyone or even looking up.

When we look down, we connect to our feelings about the present, how sad we feel now. When we look up, we see possibilities.

In order to make friends we first have to believe we can. If we approach a social situation believing we can't, then we can't.

Henry Ford famously said, "If you think you can do a thing or think you can't do a thing, you're right."

What we focus on is what we will get. So, before we do anything, we need to talk with our child about that process of going up to someone we don't know, breaking it down into bite size chunks and, most important of all, isolating that limiting belief and changing it to a resourceful belief.

Beliefs change, they really do. Just think of something you used to believe and no longer believe. What happened to make you change it? We change our beliefs through new knowledge. This is the case for your child too. Here's where you come in. Your child believes they can't make friends perhaps, can't initiate conversation or feels socially shy and awkward.

A way to help your child is to ask them to think about what other children will like about them and what makes them a good friend. How can you attract others when you don't believe in yourself? If this is relevant for your child, read the chapter on Low self-esteem.

Another way to help your child with this is to ask them, "Who do you know who has the skills you need to make friends easily?" One of the core principles of NLP is **modelling** which is when we extract another person's skills and structure along with the belief they have that enables them to do it with excellence.

Think about it this way:

> "I want to model the way that (child's name) makes friends."

How do they do it?

Observe
Listen
Be curious

What is the structure? What happens first, then, and then next?

> "If you had to guess, what do you think is the underlying belief they have about their ability to make friends?"

My guess would be that someone who makes friends easily probably believes that it is easy and your child who struggles thinks it is difficult but there may be more to it. How easy would it be to make friends if you didn't like yourself very much? What if you thought others were laughing behind your back?

Also, bear in mind that some children are perfectly happy with a few friends and may simply feel they 'should' have more for one reason or another. Perhaps they've picked up from you that they have too few friends or they see others with a crowd around them and think they should have too. This is about knowing yourself and this takes time.

Remember the NLP belief of excellence 'you already have all the resources' from Part 1?

What if your child already has the skills to achieve this but doesn't realise it?

What does making a friend involve, what skills?

Ask them.

Where do they have these skills?

Many children play sports in teams. Part of playing as a team involves making some sort of signal to another player that you are about to pass the ball (otherwise you might hit the back of their head!) so a signal starts a process: using the eyes, maybe making a sound, an action, movement. Then you pass and indicate, perhaps, that they are to pass back when you run ahead towards the goal. You indicate this again with body language. This connection is a metaphor for friendship, making connections, giving and receiving of signals. The underlying belief may be different, it's about being in a team and wanting to win in the context of sport but what if making friends could be framed like this?

In NLP we talk about chunking up and chunking down. What could be a bite size first step? How achievable is that?

Just how **RELEVANT** is it for them?

Children need to be invested in a process, they need to really want it. It is not enough for it simply to be 'nice to have'. To be relevant, the outcome needs to fit with our values in life. For a child, simply ask how important it is for them and what difference it will make.

"What will be different when you have this outcome / friend?"

It will probably affect everything in their life and give them confidence for all areas of school and home life.

Parents often worry about their child's academic progress, but if a child is lonely and unhappy, misses friendships and connection, it affects their concentration and focus on schoolwork because their emotional wellbeing is compromised.

When are they going to make some changes? This is the **TIMED** aspect.

What we are looking for here is a sense of urgency, ideally the next day.

Different ways to discuss friendship

I use a number of different techniques to explore friendship and relationship issues with children. **Art** and the use of metaphor plays a huge part. This is because asking children direct questions about friendship and relationship can seem intrusive and challenging but when we approach it indirectly by them being able to project their thoughts and feelings onto paper or characters, figures, LEGO, Moshi monsters and so on, it is so much easier for them.

A fun way to get your child talking about friendship is to use something like Moshi Monsters.

Ask them to choose which one is them, then they pick **Moshi monsters** to represent their friends. Perhaps they'd like to act out, using them, what happens in the playground. They can be the Film Director and describe the characters and what happens. It doesn't have to be a true fact – they can make up a story, of course. Remember though that they are projecting onto the plastic characters what they think would happen in the story so you will learn a lot about how they feel about each one and how they perceive themselves as part of the friendship group. If the story doesn't end well for them, you could suggest they create a different preferred ending.

Storytelling using **Story Cubes** works well, too. They can throw the cubes and make up stories for different scenarios. I usually suggest some such as: 'where you make the first move', 'where you make a friend', 'where you tell the teacher what's happening in the playground', 'where you play a game with your brother' and so on. Then when they get the idea, they can create some stories for themselves.

I like to use something like a **sand tray** to explore friendship and family dynamics. I set this up using dinosaurs, LEGO figures, Moshi monsters and any other things I can find. I say,

> "Let's use the sand tray to show me how school seems to you now."

When asking them about their sand tray use what we call 'clean questions'.

- Tell me about this character?
- Which one are you?
- What is there about that character that reminds you of you?
- What is there about the colour of this one?

Try to avoid asking 'why' questions because this is an exercise using metaphor and not the conscious mind as friendship is not necessarily very logical.

Take a photo so you can compare it afterwards because then ask them to recreate the sand tray with how school would be when they have friends.

Notice the difference, what is added, what is taken away?
Which characters move?
Ask them more questions like the first set but bear in mind that they have done the work already. Simply by creating this imaginary future they have given their mind a mental rehearsal for the outcome they desire.

If you don't have a sand tray or your child isn't keen, you can make it into an art exercise or act it out as a role play. Children who like music could write a song or a piece of music about friendship, or make a LEGO model of friendship, write a poem, or a story. The idea is to create the possibility. If your child doesn't even think it's possible and can't imagine what it might look, sound and feel like, then how can it happen?

I really like the LEGO model of friendship. I use **LEGO Serious Play** but you can use your own LEGO or bricks or other construction material, even cereal boxes. The important thing is that they're creating a concept that they need to work on but in a fun and creative way.

> "If making friends/friendship/trust (choose what you think would be most helpful for your child) was a model, what would it look like?"

As they think about it, their neural pathways are rejigging to work out how to do this thing but it's play, rather than a parent asking them or a teacher.

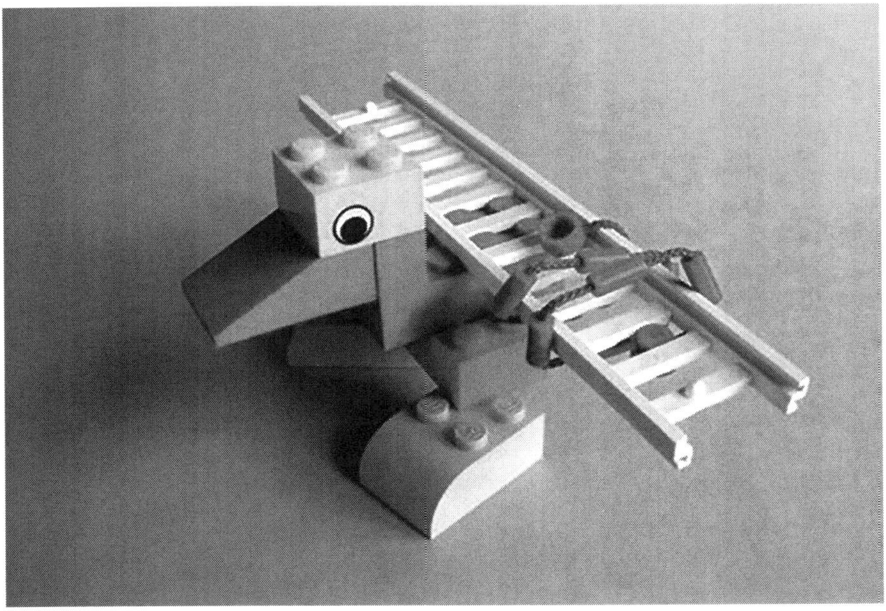

The skills they need are ones they have: walk, talk, reply, nod, smile and so on. It's the belief that's missing.

Another great technique for overcoming limiting beliefs about making friends is called Perceptual Positioning. You can also use it for bullying or fallouts with friends by putting the bully or the friend in Position 2 instead of the limiting belief. Position 2 is essentially where we put whatever is getting in the way of Position 1 getting what they want.

Preparation

Create a working space with three chairs or cushions arranged in a triangle.

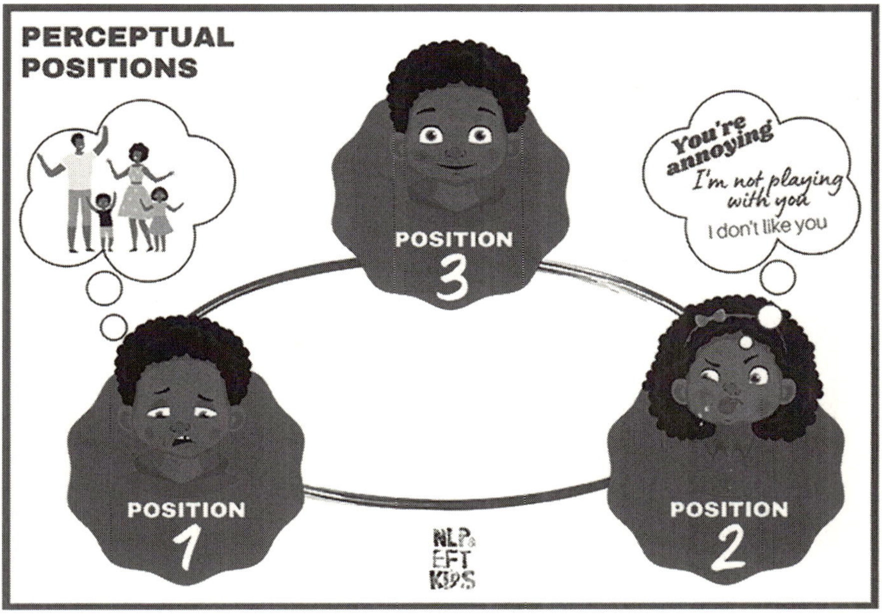

Step 1

They should decide which chair is Position 1. This is where they sit when they are themselves and from where they express their own wants and needs. They sit in that chair and think about what they want in the area of friendship. It could be about siblings of course or relationships with you, their parent. Then they speak to Position 2 and in that chair can be:

- The person they'd like to befriend
- Former friend
- A sibling or family member
- The part of them that feels they can't (their limiting belief about being able to make friends)
- The part of them that feels unlovable
- The bully

Tell Position 2 what they feel.

Position 2 is basically whatever they feel is stopping them from making friends. Obviously there isn't actually someone in the chair, it is the imagined person or feeling. Children have fantastic imagination so let them use it.

When they've said what they want to say, they should stand up and 'break state'. This means to move, dance or jiggle about and it is the best way to make sure that when they sit in position 2, they have moved out of position 1 in their head and body.

Step 2

Sit in Position 2 as that person or belief and respond to Position 1. What does Position 2 have to say? When they do this, they are connecting with that part of them that feels they can't connect to this person and by sitting in that position they are now looking at the situation from the other person's (or part of them) perception. That's why it's called perceptual positioning.

Give them time to think about this. It may be the first time they've tried to really view the situation from another perspective so resist the temptation to help them out. Yes, I do know how tempting it can be.

Once they've said something to Position 1, they should 'break state' again and return to Position 1 to respond.

Allow the conversation between Position 1 and Position 2 to continue so long as an understanding is developing. If the conversation starts to repeat itself, you can make a small intervention such as:

- What good thing is Position 2 doing for Position 1?
- In what way does Position 1 need Position 2?
- What would Position 1 have to do if Position 2 wasn't there?
- How could Position 1 reassure Position 2?

The reason we use 'Position 1' and 'Position 2' is to avoid naming people because we are focusing on the position rather than the whole person, it is a position they are taking on an issue. This enables them to see that a position can change, move, develop and be understood and appreciated.

The way we are looking to resolve this is by Position 1 gaining an understanding of Position 2 and being able to move forward now, emotionally.

Once you're there, ask your child to sit in Position 3 and just sum up what was said by each position and confirm the next step.

Another technique that helps children to understand how the dynamics of friendship and relationships work is **The Drama Triangle**.

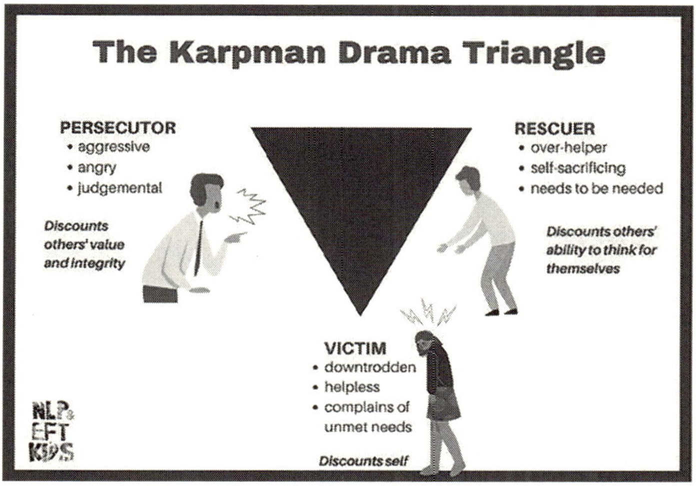

Like the perceptual positioning exercise, these are positions or roles, rather than people. Indeed, the same person often moves from feeling helpless and downtrodden, to shouting and being aggressive then moving into over-helping, then back to downtrodden. The point is that when we do this, there is no escape, we are in a process with no satisfactory outcome for anyone. No one's needs are met and no one feels seen, heard and understood.

Looking at the child represented by the Victim position, does that look like your child ever, when they go into school, worrying that no one will talk to them? We as parents may be tempted to 'rescue', maybe taking them in rather than them going by bus or walking, so we stay with them for as long as possible? Or do we get cross? We know that they have to go to school, maybe we have to get to work and this happens too often. There are no winners in this situation.

Instead, we need to do something different.

> 'If you always do what you've always done, you'll always get what you've always got.'

So to get a different outcome we have to do something different. This is about taking responsibility for ourselves rather than expecting others to change. We have no control over them, anyway.

Whoever is taking the Rescuer role needs instead to become more of a 'coach' and encourage the Victim to be a problem solver.

- What do you think?
- What could you do instead?
- What do other children do to make friends?
- What is a good way to make a friend?
- What happens when you do something else?

The person in the Persecutor role needs to acknowledge their good intent and express their needs and intention calmly and clearly. It could be you of course, we all get a turn there in this triangle at one point or another because there's only so much rescuing and victimhood that we can cope with before we explode!

The Victim needs to start thinking creatively about how to solve the problem, take responsibility for change and focus on the compelling outcome rather than all the reasons why they can't do it.

Tapping is an excellent tool for friendship, bullying, sibling rivalry and all things to do with making connections with their peers.

EFT Tapping script for friendship

Ask your child to tune in and think about the issue with their eyes closed. How does it feel? What is the feeling? Friendship can bring up all sorts of limiting beliefs about the self, such as:

- I'm not loved.
- I'm not lovable.
- No one wants to be my friend.
- I don't matter.
- I'm on my own.
- People don't like me.
- I have to get them before they get me.
- When someone gets to know me, they won't like me.

As a parent it is so tempting to dismiss these beliefs as nonsense. Your child will be worried you'll do that if they speak their fears aloud so reassure them that they can say whatever they want, and that tapping will work best when they say what they really feel.

Step 1

Ask them:

- What's the feeling?
- Where is it in the body?
- What colour is it?

- What size is it? – grape/ orange/melon or mouse/dog/elephant
- Anything else about it, texture, moving etc.

Ask them for the SUDs level. This is so we know how it's reducing as we tap.

Now we can do the set-up.

Remember, you speak first and they repeat after you, while tapping on the karate chop point.

> "Even though, I feel (feeling) in my (part of the body) and it's (colour) and (any other words they use to describe the feeling), I love and accept myself anyway."

Use a variation of this set-up statement to start the process. Remind your child that as the feeling changes or moves to a different place in the body, changes colour or any other change, they can tell you and you will change the words you use so that at all times it matches their feelings.

Step 2

Now start the tapping rounds. Starting with the top of the head and using words and phrases they've said in step 1, carry on through the points.

Top of head
Eyebrow point
Side of the eye
Under eye
Under nose
Under mouth
Collarbone
Under arm

Do several rounds, encouraging them to breathe between each round. Then check the SUDs level and the feelings. They may have changed. If so, go back and do another set-up with the new feeling and two more tapping rounds using the new words.

Continue until your child is calm and has some insight and resolution around this issue.

Lastly, encourage your child to make baby steps towards improving and building relationships and remind them that it's OK to make a few mistakes along the way, it's all a learning process.

7

Learning struggles

Whatever label may be used for some children, all children have aspects of learning that they find more difficult than others. Here are some of them:

- Sitting still
- Concentration
- Keeping quiet
- Taking turns
- Making friends
- Spelling
- Words moving on the page

If they don't struggle with the academic side of school they may still struggle with sport or the social aspects. We all have things we enjoy and things we don't, things we are good at and things we struggle with. This is normal and it's helpful to accept this rather than fight it. However, let's just navigate some of the deletions, distortions and generalisations that can get in the way of acceptance.

The first one to pay attention to is the way we **generalise**. When thinking about your child and their struggles, do you use words like *always, never, everyone, no one* or *can't*? These words ignore the exceptions – the times when they can do a thing. I've had children in my therapy room who introduce themselves like this, "I'm Joe and I've got ADHD," or "You know I'm autistic, don't you?" They generalise their struggles as if they are part of a homogenous group, all of whom have the same issues, but in my experience this just isn't the case. We are all individuals and whether we have a condition, an illness, a label, an issue, we each process our world in a unique way and need to be understood as an individual.

We also **delete** in a variety of ways which means that when your child does this through not being specific about the problems they are having, it's difficult to know how to help. So ask them for more details by using questions such as:

– When does this happen?
– Is it in every lesson, with every teacher?
– How does it happen?
– What exactly happens?
– Who does what?
– What happens first?
– Who says what to whom?
– What exactly did you say?

We **distort** by mind reading and fortune telling. Someone told a friend of mine that her daughter would never get a job because she was dyslexic. This was an error of judgement because my friend is a sports physio and has a thriving business. She's also dyslexic and studied for her qualification at a university where they could provide the learning materials in a way that meant she could learn effectively and was able to take her course in four years to allow her longer to study each module. Another friend was told that her niece would be unemployable because her ADHD made her "impossible". She's very happy working in a care home where her attention to detail is really appreciated.

The focus when children have struggles is what they struggle with and what they find difficult, but what if we looked at things another way and focused on what they find easy?

This is what we do in NLP. It's the concept of beliefs of excellence. When we know what we can do well, with ease and with excellence, we can extract the underlying belief about how we do it and look to see where we can apply that belief elsewhere in our life. You can help your child do this.

How to use **modelling** their own excellence with your child.

Ask them what they find easy, make a list. If they mention an activity, a sport or a hobby, delve deeper.

Thinking about that activity/sport/hobby, what skills, strengths or competencies enable you to do that well? What, specifically, is involved when you do that thing well?

For example, if I was thinking about tennis, my list might include: being able to move fast, anticipate where the ball would land, be strategic about where to place the ball, hit the ball hard, being able to judge how high so it goes over the net, keeping track of the score, paying attention and so on.

You may need to help them with their list.

For each skill on their list ask them what their belief is about it. Let me give you an example from my list above.

Ability	Belief
Being able to move fast	It is important to move fast so you can return the shot

When you have their list and the accompanying belief, ask them to think about how they could use that belief in another area of their life. For this it helps to think about which particular aspect of their life they'd like some help with.

We need to think about **compelling outcomes**.

What would make them happy? Another list would be great here.

When you have a few things on the list, check that they are all written as 'towards'. What I mean here is that they are things they want rather than things they don't want. They need to be written as a positive.

Now check that what they've written is in their control. If it isn't, help them change it so it is something they do have control over.

The next stage is to give each one a score out of 10 for how much they want it, so we know which outcome to focus on first. Take the highest scoring outcome and work on that.

So now let's use the SMART process to talk about their compelling outcome which will look something like this,

> "I want to be able to ...."

S – Specific

What specifically do they want to be able to do? Remember big chunk and small chunk from Part 1? It's no good having a vague mission because how would one know where to start and what success would look like?

Chunk it down to something precise and meaningful.

M – Measurable

How will they know when they have achieved it? How will it be measured?

A – Achievable

Can they do this? Is it possible?

R – Relevant

Will it matter anyway? How important is it to be able to do this?
It is only when the outcome is truly compelling that your child will invest time and effort into achieving it.

T – Timed

This means that there is a plan in terms of when they will do it, not 'at some time in the future'.

Now we have well and truly interrogated the outcome and reworded it, checked they really want it so we can go ahead and find the belief of excellence they need to be able to do it.

Write down their final compelling outcome below:

....

Now look back at the beliefs list. Ask them how they can use these beliefs to achieve their compelling outcome.

....

They may be amazed that beliefs they have associated with one area of their life can be so useful in achieving something they really want in another area of their life.

Lots of us have problems with concentration and focus. I have heard many children talk about how difficult they find it to concentrate, yet my observations of them are that their listening skills are excellent, they remember what I have said and do what I ask them to do for 'homework'. When we do the exercise above, we find that there are many examples in their life where they have concentration skills but whilst they have the belief that it matters, say, to concentrate in their video games, in their school lessons, that belief is lacking. The belief they have about the school lesson is that it is boring, doesn't matter or that they're tired or just fed up of sitting still and want to run off some energy. They have the skills but not the belief to go with it in that situation.

So how do we 'map across'? How do we take that belief and apply it where we need it?

One way is to chunk up which is to switch to the bigger picture. You can do this by saying, "so if you can use this belief to do this thing in your sport/video games etc how could you use it for this other thing you want to do?

Apart from modelling beliefs of excellence and looking at compelling outcomes, there are a number of other ways your child can improve their concentration, focus and commitment to learning at school.

Use their **imagination**. Imagine this is the most interesting lesson there could possibly be. Imagine how the topic could be of use later in life and spend time outside school hours, exploring YouTube to find other presentations of the same content, but perhaps conveyed in a way that is more fun, or more visual if they have a visual preference, or more auditory if that's their way, or more kinaesthetic if that's the way they learn best. Believe that every topic is inherently interesting if only you find just the right person to present the material in a really cool way. Make it their mission to find it!

EFT Tapping is another really good way to shift from a state of boredom, feeling like you can't do something or not wanting to do it.

Tapping script for learning struggles

Step 1

Start in the usual way by asking your child to 'tune in' to how they feel when they are trying to learn something and are struggling. Perhaps they can take themselves back to a lesson from earlier in the day or doing their homework recently when they felt like this.

- What's the feeling?
- Where is it in the body?
- What colour is that feeling?
- If it had a size, what size is it?

Let's give the issue a SUDs level, something 0-10 to represent how intense the feeling is as they tune in. If it's easier for them, ask them to describe it in terms of what size animal would it be?

Step 2

Now we can get tapping on the karate chop point.

Do the set-up first:

> "Even though I feel this .... (colour) .... (feeling) in my .... (part of the body) I love and accept myself anyway."

We do this 3 times.

Step 3

Then start the tapping rounds, tapping 6 or 7 times on each of the tapping points shown in the illustration below.

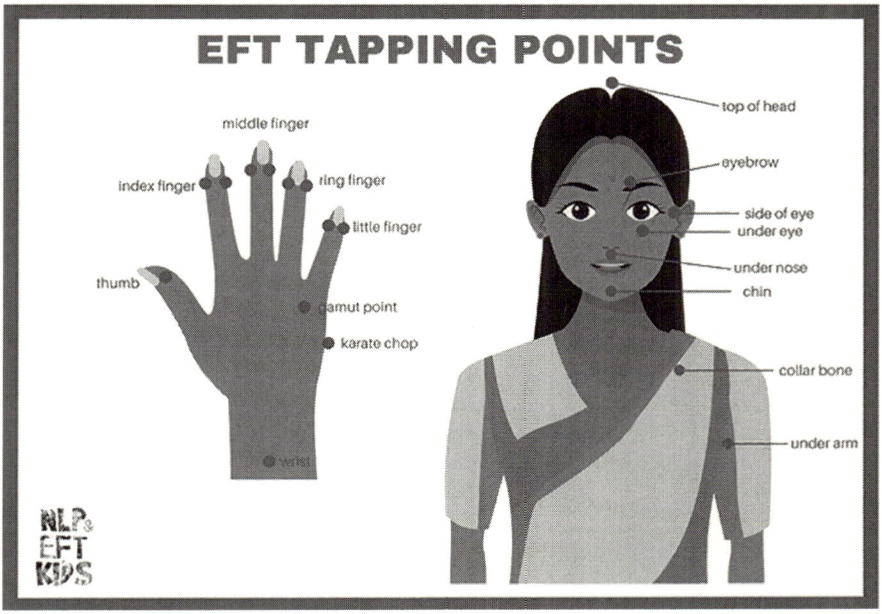

As we tap on those points, starting at the top of the head, we use some of the words your child has used to describe how they feel. You can tell them that you will be using their words, but if any of the words don't seem quite right, they should tell you so you can change them. Obviously when they are tapping for themselves they can choose and change their own words as they go. Perhaps phrases like this:

'so boring'
'can't concentrate'
'think I'm stupid'
'don't understand'
'waste of time'
'won't need to know this ever again'

And so on. What they are doing is tapping on the meridian point and saying the negative emotion that they want to clear.

When they've gone round twice, you can check whether their SUDs level has reduced. Hopefully it has.

Check whether there's been a change in the feelings. Sometimes feelings change. If you've been tapping on 'overwhelm' for example, this can change to something more specific as they are tapping round the body.

If they're tapping on 'feeling stupid' they might move to feeling cross or frustrated. As the emotion changes, so you change the words. Obviously it is most effective if they can learn to tap on their own emotions and do it whenever they feel them. This way they get a measure of control over them.

Aim for them to get down to a SUDs level of zero so they can feel relaxed and in a good learning state. Tapping can be used to clear distractions and concentrate, to feel able to learn, and to clear feelings of overwhelm and incompetence.

Schools use tapping at the start of the day to get everyone in a good learning state, clearing whatever worries they came into school with. Many use **silent tapping** so each child taps on whatever is stopping them from being in the best learning state for the day. The tapping can be repeated after breaks and after lunch so that each child has an effective means of staying focused on their lessons. Schools where tapping has been introduced have found that children spontaneously use tapping to help each other in the playground and share their new skills with their families.

You might like to do some tapping with your child each morning before they go into school to set them up for the day and remind them to use their finger tapping whenever they need to.

8

Low self-esteem

There can be quite a bit of confusion around self-esteem and confidence with children feeling one or the other and parents not always recognising the difference.

Children often feel they aren't good enough. They can't do what their peers are doing, don't look as good, don't have as many friends, feel that they are a disappointment to their parents, feel 'less than' compared to their sibling. It is a 'less than' feeling in every sense and tends to be conveyed by closed body posture, shoulders rounded, head lowered, arms static, slow movement, slow speech, low tone and lots of 'don't knows'.

They will find it difficult to accept positive feedback because they don't think they've done well enough and will always find someone who has done better or is 'more than', them.

Or perhaps they may be hesitant about initiating contact, reluctant to draw attention to themselves, won't put their hand up in class and avoids doing anything new. They don't want to be on stage, speak in class, or take a prominent role in a sports team and prefer to be on the outside of what's going on. They may simply not have a need to stand out, not have a need for social interaction and be quite comfortable in that quieter space, often alone but not necessarily lonely. They have friends but possibly just a couple and these are likely to be close friends. They aren't unfriendly with the rest of the class but they don't need to be in the centre of a big friendship group. They will mumble, rather than speak so others can hear and they will avoid eye contact.

But this does not mean that they feel 'less than'.

This chapter is for parents who know that their child is feeling 'less than.' If your child is shy, socially awkward, or lacks the skills to put themselves forward, put their hand up in class, or volunteer for tasks at school or positions of responsibility, ask them. Avoid using terminology like 'confident' or 'low self-esteem' and instead use a projective style of questioning like this.

> "If you saw a child alone in the playground, standing apart from the other children in his or her class, what do you think they're thinking?"

In essence the sort of phrases you'll hear from a child with low self-esteem are, "I'm not good enough," and, of course, "I can't."

Whereas the shy, socially awkward is more likely to say, "I don't want to," or "I can't."

Yes, that's right. Both will say, "I can't," but you'll hear more of an undertone of "I won't" from the shy child.

So another option as a parent is to ask "can't" or "won't"?

I think a good exercise to do here, especially if you're still not sure, or they are unsure, is to introduce **PTT**, picture tapping technique.

Exercise

Materials: plain paper, felt pens of every colour, including black, water.

Explaining the process to your child.

This is something we can do together to help you feel better about that thing that happened. I'm going to ask you to draw what you feel, not pictures like we have on the wall, just squiggles and things. I'm going to ask you to think about the thing that happened and just draw what you feel about it. Use these felt pens, whatever colours you like. When you're finished just tell me. I expect we'll do about 5 pictures. In between each drawing we are going to tap on different parts of our body to release the bad feelings. You may feel better after. Is that OK?

Step 1

Ask your child to 'tune in'. This means to focus on the situation they had that upset them. They need to think about the situation itself, what happened and how they felt. Avoid suggesting how they might have felt.

We need to use 'clean language' which is when we allow them to feel whatever they feel and use their own words to describe it rather than imposing our map of the world and our vocabulary which is of course going to be more mature and knowledgeable, but not necessarily an accurate representation of what they experienced.

Step 2

Once they are ready ask them to draw their feelings on the paper. The words I use are

> "If you were to draw a picture of how what happened/this situation makes you feel then what would you draw?"

Squiggles and wiggles, shapes and anything, it doesn't matter, just however they want to express these feelings. When they've stopped, ask them to write a title on the paper.

> "If this picture had a title what would it be?"

Sometimes children say they don't know. I ask them to ask the picture, "What would you like to be called?"

Sometimes they say "nothing" or "blank" and those are fine to write down as the title although I wouldn't actually suggest it unless they do.

Step 3

Now comes the tapping bit. We are going to look at the drawing and you will show your child what to do.

> "Follow me and repeat after me, what I say. If I say anything you don't agree with, tell me, ok?"

Here are the points:

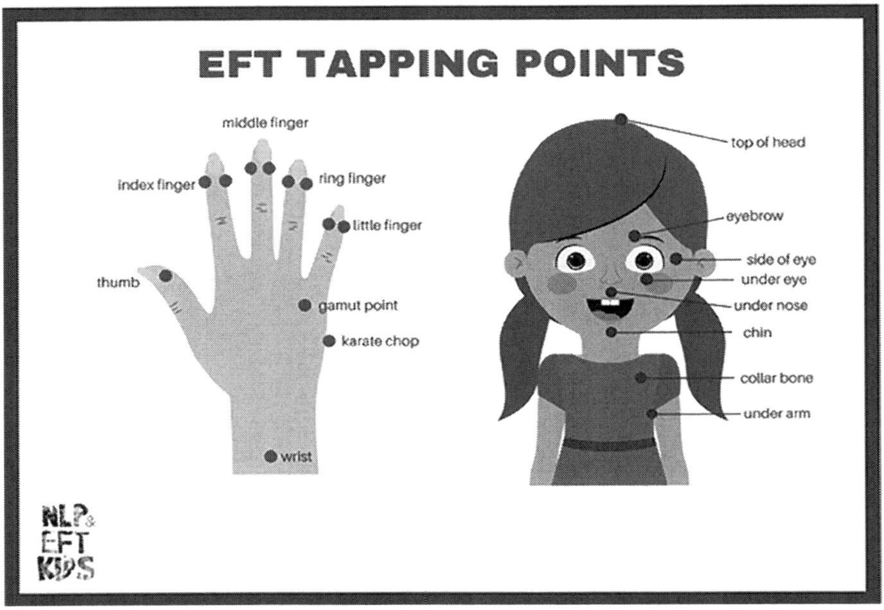

> "Even though I have drawn this picture and called it .... I love and accept myself anyway."

We say this 3 times. Make sure they breathe in between.

If they can't say that, and some find it hard, we can say:

> "Even though I have drawn this picture and called it .... I'm ok for now."

Step 4

Now we do two tapping rounds. This means that we tap around the body (see illustration above) and at each point we say something that they have drawn. We just say the colour and the shape so:

Blue circle
Red square
Yellow wiggly line
Brown star shape

So, agree with your child the colour and shape and tap seven times on each point, saying the description of each bit of their drawing. It's a factual description we need not the emotion behind it or whatever it represents because they know that, and you don't need to, in order to help them. It's just what they've drawn on the paper that we refer to.

When you've done two rounds of tapping ask them to write the number 1 on the first sheet of paper and put it to one side.

Then we do another drawing so again we 'tune in' and repeat the same process.

Step 5

Each time your child draws a picture they tune in first and then draw how they feel about the situation. Remind them that once they start to feel different, and to feel more positive, they should let you know as we only tap on the bad feelings.

You may notice a change in their physiology as they start to clear the negative feelings. Colours may get lighter, shapes might be more curvy and less jagged.

You can ask the question:

> "Does this picture represent your resolution where you're happy or is there another picture?"

It's remarkable, but I have found that whilst this might seem like quite a grown-up question and one that they might not be able to answer, in fact, they can. If they aren't sure, I ask them to look at their picture and ask:

> "Are you my resolution picture?"

Maybe they have one or two more. Children want to please and if you've said there may be 5 pictures and they've already done 5, they may want it to be the resolution picture. It's important that they find resolution. If they still seem a long way off, you can do what we call a 'forced resolution'. The advantage of this is that it gets them thinking about what might be possible in what they feel is a stuck or impossible situation. The way to do this is to ask:

> "What would you draw if this issue was completely resolved?"

So let's assume you now have a resolution picture. Remember, we don't need to know what their resolution is, nor the nature of the problem. All we need to know is that they have, with the help of their subconscious mind, resolved it. We don't tap on this resolution picture but we do give it a title. Here's what we say next:

> "Imagine you were to put a frame round this resolution picture. What colour or combination of colours would it be?"

Now we ask them to tune in, close their eyes and put both hands on their heart while you say these words:

> "I want you to imagine bringing the colour of the frame of your resolution picture through your body, coming in through your head, down through your chest, your tummy and down through your legs, singing and dancing all over your body, finding anywhere that needs special healing. Tell me when you're done and open your eyes."

I usually leave things a bit quiet after a PTT session to allow them to just enjoy the peace that resolution brings. I don't ask them anything and we may move on to chat about easy stuff for a bit.

Children with low self-esteem have often had it for as long as they can remember whereas confidence can ebb and flow depending on a number of factors such as the school year, how well they feel they are doing and the friends they have.

The reason for this is that they probably picked up the low self-belief in early childhood and it can be as a result usually of something fairly innocuous at the time. Parents and teachers can unwittingly say something or do something that can create a limiting self-belief in a child.

A good way to explore this is by using a **Time Line**.

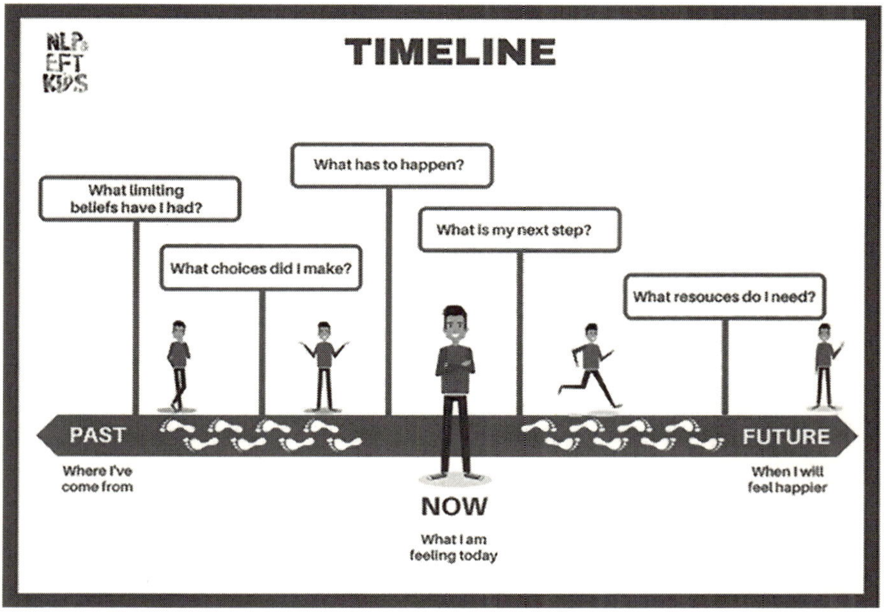

The Time Line enables a child to go back into the past and revisit key events that may have impacted their lives, ideally finding the first one where the low self-esteem started. Then we can move into the future and consider a time when they have high self-esteem and what that will be like. This exercise shows children that self-esteem does not have to be their identity; it is not a fixed state, or a fact, simply a belief that they can change with your help.

Exercise

Ask your child to imagine a line along the floor which will be their Time Line going from birth to when they will be really old, about 20. They usually love that!

Some children like to stand on the Time Line with it going 'through' them front to back and others like to stand on it with it going through the side. It doesn't matter which way they prefer. They just need to decide which end is birth and which is super old.

Ask them to stand on it at the point that represents where they are today, at their current age. It is not important that they work it out exactly! We just need a point that is the present.

I usually say, "Can you stand on a point on your Time Line that represents the present, where you are on your Time Line today?"

Ask them to tell you how they feel about themselves. I find it helps to use tapping here. Start by tuning in. We do this for most exercises because a parent may have been talking about something like friends or schoolwork and by tuning in, we refocus their mind on themselves and how they feel and away from outside matters.

To remind you, tuning in is closing the eyes, putting your hand or hands on your heart and lowering your head, as if focusing inwards on your feelings. It's helpful to take some deep breaths and drink water when you tap with your child as tapping moves the body's energy around and can make us thirsty.

Ask your child what feelings are coming up,

> "As you tune into those feelings, what words come up? They don't need to make sense."

Encourage your child to use the word 'I' as in 'I feel...' rather than what we call nominalisations which are words like *anxiety*, *anger*, or *low self-esteem*. Phrases that would indicate low self-esteem are:

> "I feel I don't matter."
> "I don't feel important."
> "I feel unlovable."

Children with low self-esteem may well not even be able to identify their feelings because they feel they don't matter.

So now, taking the karate-chop point and tapping on the side of the hand, you say, using their words:

> "Even though I don't feel important, I love and accept myself anyway."

Now your child may not love and accept themselves anyway, in fact that would be a sign that they did indeed have low self-esteem so they may prefer to say:

> "Even though I don't feel important right now, I'm a good boy/ girl and I'm OK."

We say this 3 times, with you saying the phrase and checking with them that the words fit what they feel, they repeat them each time, after you.

Ask them where the feeling is in their body and the colour, texture, size. Examples might be:

Black ball in my tummy
Red cloud in my head
Blue jelly feeling in my heart
Sick feeling in my tummy

We hold a lot of feelings in our tummy, chest, heart. You can ask size by comparing with fruit, so it might be the size of a grape, orange, melon.

So now we tap around the body using this reminder phrase. Encourage them to breathe.

Do 2 rounds and then ask them to guess what earlier age they also felt this feeling. It's important to guess rather than calculate. Just tell them to go to the age on their Time Line.

At this new place

Ask, "What has just happened when you felt this (use their words that you've been tapping on) ...?"

Ask them to step off the Time Line and face their younger self. We do not want them to re-experience what happened, we just want them to observe it as their older self, in a disassociated way, so they stay safe. So we now refer to their younger self as 'he' or 'she'.

- Where is he/she?
- Who has done or said what?
- What does your younger self make this mean?
- What decision do they make about themselves?
- What belief do they create about themselves?

You're looking for when they created the belief they have now. This age may not be the earliest and we work down the ages until we find it.

We need to heal this younger version of them. Remember, even though you are their parent, in this instance you are their coach, so hold back from fixing, explaining or clarifying. Their perception of what happened is their fact. It may not be yours and that doesn't matter. It's their perception we need to work with.

So we ask:

What do they need right now?

Their younger self may need a hug or to be told that they do matter, that they are important. Ask them who they need to hear that from and ask them to imagine doing this with them. They are working with their own inner child, their own younger self, so they will know best how to help them.

Just ask them to let you know when it's done. Check what the new belief is. Hopefully it's a healthier one but they may still need to go further back to find the earliest imprint of that belief.

Ask them to step back on the Time Line and ask their younger self what earlier age they need to go to, to clear this limiting belief.

Continue until the new belief is strong and positive.

Anchoring

Let's now anchor the new positive belief.

On the Time Line at the earliest age when you have the new belief ask your child

> "If this new belief had a colour what would it be?"

Some children may be happier with a sign like a thumbs up or a 'high five' or putting their hand to their heart. Others may like to say a word like 'I'm good' or 'Cool' or whatever they like to say when they are feeling positive. Ask them:

> "Is there something you can do to remind you of this good feeling about yourself?"

I explain an anchor like this:

Imagine you are a boat tossed around on the stormy sea. You want to feel good about yourself but things keep happening to toss you about. What if you could drop an anchor to keep you still and safe on the sea? We are going to create an anchor that you can use whenever you feel a bit unsure of yourself to remind yourself of this new belief .... use the new belief, e.g. ‘I am important’ or ‘I do matter’.

Once they have understood the process, ask them to use their anchor and gradually walk back to the place on the Time Line where they started. Are they still able to hold onto that belief? Hopefully they can.

Back on that point, check in with how they feel about themselves. Now ask them to take a step into the future along the Time Line. They may like to think about something coming up that they want to feel good about or it may just be something more general such as going back to school after the weekend or a holiday.

Once you’re sure they have imprinted and anchored the new belief, you can both stop and take a rest.

I often suggest that the child writes a letter to their younger self from their older self, telling them what they needed to hear at that younger age.

This can be a tiring and emotional process so make sure you both drink some water. You may be feeling emotional about this because you will have been involved and may not realise what happened or the significance. Allow yourself some quiet time and you may want to do some tapping yourself on your own. And that’s OK.

LEGO modelling

You can discover so much about your child's neural patterns simply by watching and listening. Actions really do speak louder than words. I use LEGO Serious Play with children and although you may not have this particular set which includes all the colours, shapes and odd pieces, you can create something similar yourself using your child's LEGO. Take the figures out because this is an exercise of metaphor so we want children to project their imagination onto the pieces rather than use figures to represent themselves. Do this ahead of time so that you have the set you want to use, all ready. It is important to have a wide range of colours of bricks because we express our feelings through colour. You don't need a vast amount, just a biscuit tin or Tupperware container will do.

Exercise

This is an exercise for talking about self-esteem but you need to go a bit broader than this in order to tease out how they feel about themselves because a child with low self-esteem in perhaps one or two areas of their life, may not feel it in all, so we don't want to zone in completely on this as if it is their identity.

Ask:

> "How could you use this LEGO to create a model of how you feel about yourself?"

Explain that you don't want a model of themselves, but a model of how they feel about themselves. There are no right or wrong answers of course.

You shouldn't give them much time because it is really their first instinctive thoughts that will more accurately represent who they are.

If it's relevant in your child's case, you can ask them to do other models:

- how they felt about themselves in their previous school;
- how they think their sibling thinks about themselves;
- how they feel about themselves when they are at their best.

When they have finished, just ask them to tell you about their model.

> "Tell me about your model."

Listen to their words and use 'clean language questions' to get them to expand.

- What is there about that green/grey/brown/yellow etc

There will be a reason subconsciously why they have chosen that colour. Not logically, perhaps, although it could be logical. If they need a bit more help here, try:

> "If that colour represented a feeling, what would it be?"
> "What does that colour remind you of?"
> "When you think about that colour, what comes to mind?"

- What is there about that shape?

I know LEGO bricks are rectangular but hopefully you've found bits that are square, long strips, flat pieces and so on. If you have, you can explore the significance of shape. You may also have found pieces like windows or doors to use, these are quite useful to talk about as you can imagine.

- What is there about the height, width, arrangement of the LEGO pieces?

Is their model tall, short, long, wide? Is it a bit unstable? Is it quite solid? What is their feeling about this?

- If their model could talk, what would it say?

This is a way of further projecting themselves onto the model. You can even get them to have a conversation with their model by asking:

"And what would you say back to them?"

- What does your model need in order to feel even better about themselves?

Ask them to add whatever they need in the way of other LEGO pieces and remove any they want, in order to create a model that feels better about itself.

This is a very interesting aspect of the exercise because it introduces them to the idea that they can change whatever they like about their self-belief, a life-changing revelation.

Self-belief is not a fact.

Look at the bits they remove, can you remember what the colour represented? Can you remember what that piece was and what it meant?

Look at the bits they replace them with. Are the colours brighter? Probably. This is why having all the colours is important.

Now go through the questions above based on the new model.

Then ask the questions below:

- What has changed?
- What were the bits they needed?
- What needs to happen in order to make this model their reality?
- What do they need to do?
- What is the first step they could take to achieve this model?

It is very important that they understand that this is their responsibility and that you step back from fixing and sorting for them. This whole book is designed to turn you into a coach and simply to guide your children, to support and encourage but leave them to take responsibility for the changes because they can .... remember, they already have all the resources.

It's a good idea to take a photo of their new model because they might like to put a picture on the wall of their room to remind them of what they want to feel about themselves.

I love working with LEGO. As children think about what they're creating, knowing it is a model from their own imagination and reflecting a part of themselves, they are tapping into their own 'inner knowing' and reflecting on new possibilities. It's easy to change a LEGO model. What if it were easy to change their neural pathways and experience a new self-belief that was better and more empowering than the old one?

Superhero exercise

This is another great exercise.

What child doesn't want to secretly become a superhero and be able to be the best version of themselves just like that?

I use Elitsa Velikova's Art Therapy Cards.

Take the Superhero one or just ask them:

> "Draw yourself as a superhero."

Explain that you don't mean them to draw an existing superhero, they should come up with their own superhero.

Make sure they have plenty of different colour felt pens, paints or crayons.

Use Elitsa's questions.

> "What are the superpowers this hero possesses and what can they do with them?
> "For what or whom are those superpowers designed?"
> "Does the hero have a special mission?"
> "What is the special suit of the hero?"
> "Where does this hero live?"
> "Is there a trusted friend/assistant/buddy/partner for the hero?"
> "What is the name of the hero?"
> "What are the personality traits of the hero?"
> "Do you find any of these qualities in yourself?"
> "Are there any qualities in this hero you would like to develop in yourself?"

I then go on to bring the superhero to life by asking them how school will be different with these superhero powers, when they will use them, in which lessons, with which teachers, with which children.

How will they use them at home? What will be different?

How could they use their qualities? What will happen when they let their superhero qualities shine their light?

What about their personality traits? Which ones will make the most difference? What will their friends notice? What will teachers notice? What will Mum and Dad and their siblings notice?

We can then use the Circle of Excellence exercise to create a lovely anchor for them.

Exercise

Ask your child to imagine a circle in front of them. This is their **Circle of Excellence**.

Explain that when you say 1-2-3-go, they will step into it and do their superhero pose as they think about all those superpowers, qualities, personality traits that their superhero possesses.

When you see them slightly lose that connection or feeling, they should step back out. We need to build association between the circle and the superhero.

When they step out, we do a 'break state', a little dance to break the state between stepping into the circle.

Then repeat 1-2-3-go, and step into the circle to create that superhero pose again. Yes, it can be a different pose, of course.

Break state when they come out.

Repeat. Remember to break state each time.

Now, outside their imaginary circle ask them to make a circle with their thumb and index finger. The bend down and imagine scooping up their Circle of Excellence and then putting it in their pocket. This is their portable Circle of Excellence. They can use it whenever they need to be their own superhero.

I will now **Future Pace** this, which means that we imagine how the future will be with this Circle of Excellence, what will be different?

Ask them when they will use their portable Circle of Excellence. Maybe they have something coming up at school which they might find a bit challenging, some tests, new experiences, changes that they feel uncomfortable about?

"What will be different now you have your portable Circle of Excellence?"

You can extend this further still as a writing exercise.

Exercise

What if your superhero wrote you a letter? What would he or she say?

If your child has something on their mind, an event or situation that you know will be a struggle for them, ask them to write a letter to themselves as their superhero.

Dear ....

....

....

....

From .... your superhero

Psychological Reversal

Sometimes it happens that children get some positive benefit from their low self-esteem. This might sound crazy, but hear me out.

What happens when your child says, "I'm useless", "No one loves me", "I don't have any friends", "I'm not good enough"?

Of course, you give them attention. What parent wouldn't? It's natural. We can't bear to think of our child having low self-esteem. Maybe we blame ourselves. Perhaps we aren't praising them enough? Perhaps we're working too hard? Are we having to pay more attention to another sibling right now?

Be curious.

If you feel your child may have low self-esteem, start challenging yourself to look for signs of high self-esteem or whatever you deem to be the opposite, what you'd like to see. Beware of looking for confidence because, as I explained, confidence may not be their desired state. How would they like to feel about themselves? This is certainly a discussion that it's important to have.

Let's say they want to feel 'good enough.' That's a healthy outcome, as having high self-esteem may seem a bit arrogant and not what they, or you, want.

So be observant, look out for signs that they feel 'good enough', 'loved', 'heard', 'seen' and mark them out.

> "I hear you."
> "I see you."
> "I love you."
> "You are important to me."
> "You matter to me."
> "You are a good boy/girl."

What we pay attention to is what we get more of. Where we put our attention is what improves because ultimately children need your attention so instead of looking up and paying them attention for their feelings of low self-esteem, help them build their self-esteem, help them see their qualities and who they are that you love.

Vision Board

I think it's a nice idea to help your child create a vision board. This is a collage of pictures from magazines or photos, it can even be from things from the beach or the garden.

> "I want you to cut out and stick onto this sheet, images, colours, words, photos that make you feel good about yourself, positive and vibrant, full of positive energy about who you are."

Let them gather the bits first and then get the glue out to arrange them on the paper. This is because this exercise gets them thinking about who they are and they often move things about, take pictures off and want to add new ones so it's best to wait until they have completely decided before gluing them down.

It's good if you can laminate it and put it on their bedroom wall or on their door so that they see it before they set off for school.

Whatever exercises you've done with them, I think this is a good consolidation exercise.

You may want to repeat it each term because children change so much and need new images to reflect who they are now.

You may even want to do one yourself.

9

Sleep Issues

Who has the sleep problem? It is important to first decide whose problem it is because I have sometimes been told that a child has a sleep problem only to find that the child is reluctant to resolve it because the benefits are more attractive than the problem.

Now I'm not saying that this is the case in your situation and sometimes things can start one way, with the child simply enjoying that extra time with Mummy or Daddy or it can start another way with a genuine nightmare or being scared of the dark or being alone, but when things have continued to become a pattern we need to examine quite closely whose problem it is. It is then up to that person to do the work.

I'm going to cover working with a parent and working with a child here so you have both.

First, though, I want you to think back to the first time the behaviour happened. What was going on at that time?

Children will be sensitive to situations in the family or in your relationship, that you may think you're covering up really well. Death of a grandparent, for example, can affect a child more than you'd expect. Their world is very small and their parents and grandparents are people of influence so they will have a huge impact. If, when a grandparent dies, they feel they can't express their grief because they can see you are upset, they will find other ways to get the extra attention they need. If this behaviour and the associated attention gives them that comfort, the habit may continue because it's now become a pattern that feels reassuring.

So, think about when it started. What happened just before? You may need to spend time discussing that with them and allowing them time now to express that grief or loss.

What happens is that a situation, issue or event can get associated with a behaviour such that until the issue is resolved, the behaviour will continue.

Children get stuck in patterns of behaviour that become reassuring because they are familiar and they can't imagine another option. We can use visualisation to help with this. First, it's helpful to know if your child is visual, auditory or kinaesthetic. A visual child notices what they see, they have great imagination, tend to be very creative and will be the first to notice if you change your appearance in any way. An auditory child will be more verbal, chatty, will probably love music and notice sounds and what's said rather than what they see. A kinaesthetic child is active, fidgety and wants to be on the move.

Their language patterns will be different. Even if you find your child may have aspects of all three – visual, auditory and kinaesthetic – they will have a preference. Visual children tend to use words like look, see, imagine, watch, notice. Auditory preferences will be; sound, noise, hear, listen. Kinaesthetic preference will be any action or 'doing' word. Kinaesthetic children tend to be more physical too, wanting touch and cuddles. Comfort is very important so being too hot or cold in bed will affect them.

The reason I'm telling you about this is that it will help you know what to say to reassure them and to know what their focus is likely to be. An auditory child will notice every little creak and noise in the house. A visual child is likely to be more aware of the dark or indeed, light coming through a blind or curtain in the summer when they are trying to sleep and a kinaesthetic child will notice an uncomfortable bed, being too hot or cold or will want the extra cuddles.

When reassuring them, pay attention to their language pattern, for example:

Visual child

- I'd like to see you tucked up in bed with the light off when I look in on you later
- Have a look at your clock when you wake up, if it's a number smaller than 7, read your book or draw a picture and I'll look at it when I see you

Auditory child

- I can hear that you are not in bed yet, I told you it's time for bed, did you hear me?
- Can you tell me when you're ready for me to say goodnight

Kinaesthetic child

- Get into bed, get a move on, you can do it! I'll come in for a cuddle when you're in bed
- How quickly can you get ready for bed, shall I time you?

Obviously you know your own child so you can create your own versions with which to experiment.

Do your children believe you when you either threaten them or bribe them? Do they take you seriously when you tell them you want them to go to bed?

I've noticed that parents talk very differently to their children than to colleagues at work and of course they do, it's natural. However, when your child is not listening or is not doing what you've asked, it's a good idea to test out your work voice! After all, if you always do what you've always done, you will always get what you've always got. The difference is the belief behind the voice. Your work voice is delivered with the belief that you will be heard and what you ask will be done. Is your home voice asking your child to go to bed, delivered with the belief that it won't be listened to and what you ask will be ignored?

Have a go at this yourself.

Use the voice recorder on your smartphone and record various versions of an instruction regarding the going to bed routine or the waking up during the night and not going back to sleep routine, whichever you have problems with.

Version 1 – How you normally say it (you may want to check with your partner if this is how you say it).

Version 2 – How you would say it, if you were asking someone to do something at work.

Version 3 – With the belief that you deserve to be heard and that you expect to be obeyed.

Listen back to your recordings. What do you notice? Experiment with them and perfect the most effective rendition.

Remember, making good eye contact is important and combine it with your child's preferred language pattern.

Do you tell them what you DO want or what you DON'T want?

Example

I had a client who came to see me, very tired. Her daughter came into their room every night, got into their bed so she ended up sleeping on the floor because her daughter's bed was too small.

She said, "Every night when I put her to bed, I tell her DO NOT COME INTO OUR ROOM, but every night she does."

"What do you want her to do?" I asked.

She repeated that she did not want her to come into their room.

I then said, "If you always do what you've always done, you'll always get what you've always got". But still she insisted that she did NOT want her daughter to come into their room.

It's easy to get stuck in a rut, focusing on what you don't want and it can be hard to change.

I had to make it really clear before she eventually got it. I said, "I know you don't want her to come into your room, but what DO you want instead?"

At last she realised and said, "I suppose I want her to stay in her own room". I asked if she'd ever asked her to do that and she admitted that she hadn't.

The next day, she sent me an email confirming that her daughter had stayed in her own room for the first time and everyone had woken up feeling refreshed for a change.

It is much easier for children to follow what we call a 'towards' instruction of what we DO want.

If you don't believe me...

...DON'T THINK ABOUT PINK ELEPHANTS!

What are you thinking about?

Exactly.

Have you heard of the Five Love Languages? I love this and a lovely exercise you can do with the children is to find out which is their love language.

Exercise

Ask them to draw a big rectangle using up most of an A4 sheet of paper. This is their love tank. They need some different colour felt pens.

Now divide up the tank by how much of each of the following makes them feel loved. A full love tank is what we all need.

You can fill it with all of these in whatever quantity you need in order to feel loved.

Gifts – things, basically!
Physical touch – hugs and cuddles, kisses, etc.
Quality time – spending time with someone doing things together, chatting or just hanging out.
Acts of service – having things done for you.
Words of affirmation – being told that you are great.

Notice in your child's drawing which of these is the largest layer in the tank, and notice the second largest.

When you know what fills your child's love tank this will help you to know how to help them with their sleep problems.

If physical touch is not very important to them, spending time giving them hugs at bedtime isn't going to be as effective as something they need more of such as words of affirmation. Perhaps they worry about things that have happened during the day at school and your reassurance may be just what they need to settle their busy mind.

Similarly, if they want quality time, that might work as a better bribe than a gift, "Please stay in your room tonight so I can get some sleep, so we can go to the park tomorrow together."

Personally, I am a great fan of mindfulness for getting to sleep and many of my clients have successfully changed their lives by introducing this to their kids.

So many children experience waves of worries from the moment their head hits the pillow. Worries about what happened today, what might happen tomorrow, fears about what might be said, what other children will do. Children are either in the past, thinking about past events over which they no longer have any control, or future events that may not even happen. What mindfulness does, is bring them to the present moment, the now.

We can control the 'now'. We just sit in it and anything that is not now is noticed and waved away as not needed. It will still be there after our meditation but for now we are just going to be.

You can download meditation apps, meditations on YouTube. There are certainly lots available but I think for a young child, it's good to show them yourself and meditate together. After all, what's not to like. You get to meditate and clear the past day and whatever happened, you show them how to do it and you share that lovely quality time together.

What you're also doing, which I love, is that you are showing them how to self-soothe, how to do self-care. The fact that you are doing it, too, shows them the model of excellence. It can be a good family practice.

You'll find that apps like Headspace have a kids section and different topics so children can meditate on friendship, low self-esteem, anxiety and so on.

If you prefer something more self-guided consider something like a Body Scan meditation which allows you to mentally scan your body and relax any tension you find in every part of it.

What you're doing here is stilling the mind.

Another fun thing to do at bedtime is to use a mindfulness jar. Here's how to make it. You will need different colours of glitter.

Exercise

Take an empty jam jar with a lid and fill it with water, just below the top.

Talk to your child about the thoughts they have at bedtime. It's best to make the mindfulness jar at that time so they can tell you about their thoughts because they might only happen at that time.

Ask them as they mention each thought or emotion to choose a glitter colour to represent it and tip an amount into the water to represent the amount of that emotion in their mind when they go to bed.

Once they've gone through all the feelings and are satisfied that all their feelings are in the jar, they should put the lid on tightly.

Now ask them to shake the jar. This is like all their busy thoughts buzzing about when they are trying to get to sleep. As they watch all the glitter flying around in the water, ask them to notice how the glitter is settling on the bottom and the water is becoming clear again. This is just like their thoughts and emotions. By staying still and calm, breathing and waiting for the water to clear, they will soon be able to get to sleep.

By far the fastest way to get children to sleep is to teach them breathing techniques. As we count our *in* breath and our *out* breath:

In .... one two three four five six
Out .... one two three four five six

We are unable to think of anything else and that rhythmic breathing will soon get us to sleep.

But what if it doesn't?

Tapping could be the answer, especially if your child has something playing on his mind.

EFT Tapping has been described in the introduction so hopefully you read about it already. In a nutshell, it is an energy healing modality based on the energy meridians in the body. The idea is that your child says what's stopping them getting to sleep while tapping through the tapping points. So here's a great global script for you, and by global, I mean that this covers general 'not being able to get to sleep' situations but feel free to change the words to suit your own child:

Tapping script for sleep issues

Step 1

We start, as ever with a tune in and a set-up.

Let's assume your child has already said, "Mummy/Daddy I can't get to sleep." You go in and say, "OK, let's start tapping."

The words to use as you both tap on the side of your hand – the karate-chop point, are:

> "Even though I can't get to sleep, I'm a good boy/girl."

You do this 3 times tapping all the time on that fleshy part between the base of your little finger and your wrist.

Step 2

You then move on to the tapping rounds, tapping through the fingers as that's easier at night lying in bed, than tapping on the body points. So gently squeeze the top of each finger, either side of the nail.

As you do this, use your child's words, saying one word or phrase on each finger.

> "It's dark."
> "I feel all alone."
> "I'm not tired."
> "I'm scared."

Or if they just don't know why they can't get to sleep, just say:

> "I can't get to sleep."

As they breathe and tap, they will soon feel sleepy and will certainly feel calmer and closer to being able to settle. Remind them that if they do wake up, they can just tap again until they fall back to sleep.

Let's finish this chapter with a **self-compassion break**.

Show them how to put their hands to their heart and say:

> "I can't get to sleep" or whatever they are feeling right now.

Then, put their hands out in front of them outstretched, palms up as if offering this problem to the universe.

> "Right now, all over the world there are thousands, even millions of children who can't get to sleep, children just like me, I'm part of a universe of children who can't get to sleep."

This helps them realise they are not alone and lots of children struggle to get to sleep (lots of adults do too).

Then ask them to put their hands back to their heart and say:

> "What I need now is..." and they say what they need now but they don't have to say this out loud. It's just about acknowledging that they can self soothe by thinking about what they need.

To finish, ask them to imagine how great they'll feel when they wake up in the morning, refreshed, happy and looking forward to the day.

It might help if they finish with a gratitude diary to review what's been good about the day or what they're looking forward to tomorrow. Lots of children find writing their thoughts and feelings very helpful as it acknowledges them but keeps them private if they'd prefer not to share them with you.

Index